GARY MEHIGAN

Gary Mehigan is an award-winning Melbourne-based restaurateur with two decades of experience as a chef. He started his career in London, then moved to Melbourne in 1991, where he worked in a number of prominent restaurants such as Browns, Burnham Beeches Country House and Hotel Sofitel. He opened Fenix in 2000, followed by The Maribyrnong Boathouse in 2005. Gary is a household name across Australia because of his role as a judge on *MasterChef Australia* and *Junior MasterChef Australia*. Gary is the author of *Comfort Food* and the co-author, with George Calombaris, of *Your Place or Mine?* and *Cook With Me*.

LANTERN COOKERY CLASSICS

GARY MEHIGAN

LANTERN
an imprint of
PENGUIN BOOKS

STARTERS, SIDES AND SMALL BITES

MAINS

SWEET THINGS

BASICS

STARTERS, SIDES AND SMALL BITES

Pumpkin soup

This soup is a winner, mainly because it reminds you that sometimes the simplest things are the best. Grating the pumpkin helps to draw out its natural sweetness, and grated pumpkin also cooks more quickly, which helps to preserve the true pumpkin flavour. The key is to cook the pumpkin quickly, extracting the natural sugars as it softens.

You can also leave out the milk and simply blend the pumpkin to make the most beautiful puree to enjoy with roast chicken or stir through a luscious risotto.

1 × 1.6 kg jap pumpkin, peeled, seeded and cut into manageable chunks for grating
125 g unsalted butter, chopped
50 ml vegetable oil
1 teaspoon table salt
1 litre milk
sea salt flakes and freshly ground black pepper
crusty bread or garlic toasts, to serve

1 Grate the pumpkin with a coarse box grater or use the grater attachment of a food processor.

2 Heat the butter and oil in a large heavy-based saucepan over medium heat. Add the pumpkin and sprinkle with salt. Cook the pumpkin, covered, gently over low heat for 8 minutes, stirring occasionally until it is soft. To test whether the pumpkin is cooked, place a few pieces on a wooden spoon and squeeze with your thumb; they should be quite mushy. Stir in the milk and bring to the boil.

3 Blend the pumpkin mixture in a food processor or blender until creamy and smooth. Season to taste with salt and pepper. Serve with good-quality crusty bread or garlic toasts.

Chicken and white bean soup

A good chicken soup is the ultimate pick-me-up,
The chicken and stock are the essence of this soup,
so feel free to vary the vegetables from season to
season, and to replace the beans with a grain such
as rice, barley or freekah.

When cooking dried cannellini beans, I rinse
them well first as they can be quite dirty. I don't
add salt to the pan as I cook them as this toughens
them, but instead, I season them at the end of
cooking. If you can't find Tuscan black cabbage,
then use shredded silverbeet or kale instead.

1 × 1.25 kg free-range chicken
1 litre Chicken Stock (see page 134)
2 cups (500 ml) water
150 g dried cannellini beans, well washed
    and drained
1 fresh bay leaf
2 sprigs thyme
70 ml extra virgin olive oil, plus extra for drizzling
2 cloves garlic, peeled and finely chopped
1 carrot, finely chopped
1 onion, finely chopped
2 sticks celery, finely chopped
1 bunch cavolo nero (see page 139),
    washed and roughly shredded
1 handful of green beans, trimmed and sliced
1 cup (120 g) frozen or fresh peas
sea salt flakes and freshly ground black pepper
chargrilled sourdough bread, to serve

1 Place the chicken in a large saucepan or stockpot
and cover with the stock and water, then add the
cannellini beans and bring to a gentle simmer
over medium heat. Add the bay leaf and thyme,
then cook over low heat for 50 minutes or until the
chicken is cooked and the beans are tender. Remove
from the heat and leave to stand for 15 minutes.
Remove the chicken and beans from the stock and
set aside. Strain the stock and reserve. When the
chicken is cool enough to handle, remove the skin
and shred the meat from the bones into bite-sized
pieces. Set aside.

2 Meanwhile, rinse the pan and return it to
the stove. Heat the olive oil over medium heat,
then add the garlic and fry for 30 seconds or until
golden. Add the carrot, onion and celery and cook
for a further 2–3 minutes. Return the stock, beans
and chicken to the pan and bring to the boil, then
simmer for 10 minutes. Add the black cabbage and
beans and cook for a further 3 minutes, then add
the peas and cook for another 1 minute. Season to
taste with salt and pepper.

3 Ladle the soup into bowls, then drizzle with olive
oil and serve with chargrilled sourdough to the side.

Mushroom bruschetta with soft-poached eggs

Good bruschetta, like a good pizza base, should be the vehicle for showcasing great ingredients at their seasonal best. I start with a crusty, dense sourdough with loads of flavour. When it comes to toppings, grilled asparagus, buffalo mozzarella, good-quality ham, smoked trout or soft figs are just some of the fabulous options. In the height of summer, one of my all-time-favourites is to stand by the barbecue armed with a couple of garlic cloves, great extra virgin olive oil, sea salt flakes and cut ripe tomatoes, then squish and drizzle these onto the charred bread. Here I've chosen to use gutsy garlic-infused mushrooms, paired with perfectly soft-poached eggs to make a substantial brekky.

¼ cup (60 ml) olive oil
2 large cloves garlic, thinly sliced
4 slices dense sourdough bread
table salt
¼ cup (60 ml) white-wine vinegar
4 free-range eggs
freshly ground white pepper
300 g mixed exotic mushrooms, such as enoki, oyster and wood ear, trimmed
2 large portobello or king brown mushrooms, trimmed, thickly sliced
25 g unsalted butter
2 tablespoons shredded flat-leaf parsley

1 Heat the oil in a non-stick frying pan over medium heat. Cook the garlic for 2–3 minutes or until light-golden and crisp. Remove the garlic from the pan, then drain on paper towel. Pour the oil into a small bowl, leaving a little in the pan, then set aside.

2 Grill the bread on a chargrill pan or barbecue grill-plate over high heat and keep warm.

3 Bring a saucepan of water to the boil over high heat, then add a pinch of salt and the vinegar. Make sure that the water is gently boiling at a simmer. Working quickly, crack one egg at a time into the simmering water, leaving a little space between each egg. Poach the eggs for 3–4 minutes. Gently lift the eggs from the water with a slotted spoon, then drain on paper towel and season with a pinch of salt and pepper.

4 Meanwhile, heat the non-stick frying pan over high heat. Add the mushrooms and fry for 4 minutes or until golden, then add the butter and cook for another 1 minute. Add the parsley and remove from the heat.

5 Divide the mushrooms and eggs between the warm toast, sprinkle with the crisp garlic, then drizzle with a little of the reserved garlic-infused oil and serve.

Chicken liver parfait with toast

I have tried many chicken liver pate or parfait recipes in my time but this is the best – silky-smooth and packed with flavour. It's very rich so have just a little at a time and savour it. Buy super-fresh chicken livers and make sure you trim off all the connective tissue. You'll need to get started on this the day before you wish to serve it.

250 g chicken livers
½ cup (125 ml) milk
2 tablespoons olive oil
6 golden shallots, thinly sliced
1 clove garlic, peeled
50 ml Madeira
100 ml port
50 ml brandy
3 free-range eggs
1½ teaspoons table salt
½ teaspoon freshly ground white pepper
250 g unsalted butter, at room
    temperature, chopped
boiling water, for cooking
melted butter, to seal

TOAST
1 sourdough ficelle (small baguette),
    thinly sliced lengthways
melted butter, for brushing
sea salt flakes

1 To clean the chicken livers, remove the little pieces of sinew in the middle of each one. Rinse the livers under cold water and soak in the milk in the fridge overnight.

2 Heat the olive oil in a saucepan over low heat. Fry the shallots for a few seconds. Add the garlic, Madeira, port and brandy and cook over low heat for another 3–4 minutes or until reduced by two-thirds. Set aside to cool.

3 Preheat a fan-forced oven to 180°C (200°C conventional).

4 To make the toast, brush the sourdough slices with a little butter, then sprinkle with salt. Place on a baking tray and bake for 4–5 minutes or until golden. Leave to cool and set aside.

5 Drain the chicken livers and blend in a food processor until smooth. Add the eggs and blend to incorporate, then add the shallot reduction and season with the salt and pepper.

6 Place the butter in a large heatproof bowl. (The butter must be very soft – almost melting – as it is important that the butter and liver puree are at the same temperature, otherwise the butter will curdle the mixture as it stiffens. To test, dip your index finger into the butter and then into the liver puree.) Add the puree to the butter and whisk it through until the mixture has a smooth consistency. If the butter sets or curdles the mixture, warm it very gently over a pan of simmering water over low heat, whisking continuously until it smooths out.

7 Preheat the fan-forced oven to 120°C (140°C conventional).

8 Divide the mixture among two 500 ml-capacity airtight glass jars. Place the jars in a deep baking dish or roasting pan filled with enough hot water to reach halfway up the side of the jars. Cook in the oven for 45 minutes or until the parfait has set. (If you have a meat thermometer, the internal temperature should be 60°C.)

9 Remove the jars from the oven, then pour a 2–3 mm-deep layer of melted butter over the top of each parfait to seal. Seal the jars, then leave to cool and place in the fridge. Serve the parfait with the toast. Once the seal is broken, the parfait will keep in the fridge for 4–5 days.

Pork rillettes with cherry compote

Rillettes are a fabulous way to use the secondary cuts of meat – in this case, pork belly. In days of old, rillettes were preserved and stored for the harsh winter months. Imagine a little rillettes spread on toast before a hard day's work out in the fields. In fact, forget the fields – that sounds perfect right now! Classic French recipes like this make good sense – salty, fatty pork plus the acidic vinegar punch of cornichons equals edible gorgeousness. You will need to start making this the day before you wish to serve it.

800 g boneless pork belly, skin removed
35 g rock salt
4 sprigs thyme
10 juniper berries, crushed
5 white peppercorns, crushed
300 g minced pork fat
1 star anise, crushed
½ stick cinnamon
3 fresh bay leaves
3 cloves garlic, peeled
½ cup (125 ml) water
sea salt flakes and freshly ground white pepper
toasted sourdough baguette and cornichons
    (see page 139), to serve

CHERRY COMPOTE
500 g cherries, pitted
½ stick cinnamon
1 star anise
6 juniper berries
4 white peppercorns
¼ vanilla pod, split
60 g caster sugar
1 tablespoon raspberry vinegar
2 tablespoons kirsch (cherry brandy)

1 To make the cherry compote, place the cherries in a small heavy-based saucepan, then add the cinnamon, star anise, juniper berries, peppercorns, vanilla pod, sugar, vinegar and kirsch. Slowly bring the mixture to the boil over medium heat. Reduce the heat to low and simmer gently for 20 minutes. Remove the pan from the heat and set aside to cool. (Makes about 1½ cups. Cherry compote will keep in an airtight container in the fridge for up to 1 week.)

2 Place the pork belly on a baking tray, then sprinkle with the rock salt, thyme, juniper berries and peppercorns, making sure that the belly is coated on both sides. Cover with plastic film and refrigerate for 6 hours. Brush off the salt, herbs and spices, then rinse the pork under cold running water to remove any remaining salt and pat dry with paper towel.

3 Preheat the oven to 140°C fan-forced (160°C conventional).

4 Place the pork belly and pork fat in a heavy-based saucepan, then add the star anise, cinnamon, bay leaves, garlic and water. Put the lid on, then roast for 3½ hours or until the pork is tender (it must fall apart when you push a fork through it).

5 Remove the pork belly from the pork fat and set aside on a plate to cool. Strain the pork fat through a fine-mesh sieve and set aside. When the pork belly is cool enough to handle, shred the meat finely with your fingers, pulling apart the fibres. Place the shredded pork in a bowl and beat well with a wooden spoon to further break down the meat fibres. Mix a little of the fat with the pork at a time, beating with a wooden spoon to combine thoroughly. Season with salt and pepper, if required, then cover with plastic film and place in the fridge to cool. Divide the rillettes among small jars or ramekins, then cover.

6 Serve the rillettes with toasted sourdough baguette, cornichons and the cherry compote alongside. Store leftover rillettes in the fridge for up to 1 week.

Brandade with capsicum confit

Salt cod-based dishes such as French brandade and Spanish baccala crop up all over Europe. While brandade is traditionally made with salt cod, I use fresh blue-eye trevalla that I salt in the fridge overnight.

If you want to save a few hours, reduce the time allocated for salting the fish. I prefer to salt it longer because it draws out moisture, intensifying the flavour and reducing the weight of the fish. Leftover brandade can be stored in an airtight container in the fridge for up to 5 days.

30 g rock salt
1 × 180 g blue-eye trevalla fillet, skin removed, pin-boned and patted dry
1 potato
1 cup (250 ml) milk
2 sprigs thyme
2 fresh bay leaves
½ teaspoon white peppercorns
50 ml extra virgin olive oil
1½ cloves garlic, peeled and crushed
50 ml pouring cream
chargrilled or toasted sourdough bread or brioche, to serve

CAPSICUM CONFIT

2 red capsicums (peppers)
3 teaspoons olive oil
½ clove garlic, sliced

1 Sprinkle half of the rock salt onto a plate, then place the fish on top and sprinkle with the remaining rock salt. Cover with plastic film and leave in the fridge overnight.

2 Preheat a fan-forced oven to 160°C (180°C conventional).

3 Place the potato directly onto an oven shelf and bake for 45 minutes or until soft. Scoop out the flesh and set aside next to the stove to keep warm.

4 Meanwhile, to make the capsicum confit, place the capsicums on a sheet of foil on a baking tray, then drizzle with the olive oil and sprinkle with garlic. Draw up the sides of foil to enclose, then place in the oven with the potato for 30 minutes. Remove the capsicums and cool for 10 minutes. Cut the capsicums in half, then discard the seeds and cut the flesh lengthways into rough pieces. Transfer to a serving bowl and pour over the oily roasting juices, then set aside.

5 Rinse the fish, then pat dry with a paper towel. Place in a heavy-based saucepan. Add the milk, thyme, bay leaves and peppercorns. Bring to a gentle simmer over medium heat, then cook for 3–4 minutes. Drain the fish, discarding the herbs and peppercorns and reserving 50 ml of the strained milk. Crumble the fish finely between your fingers.

6 Heat half of the olive oil in a heavy-based saucepan over low heat, then add the garlic and whisk for 1 minute until fragrant. Add the fish and continue whisking over the heat until the oil has been absorbed. Gradually add the remaining olive oil. Add the potato, then the reserved milk and whisk vigorously until creamy. Remove from the heat and whisk in the cream.

7 Serve the warm brandade with the sourdough or brioche and the capsicum confit to the side.

Escabeche of mackerel

This dish can be prepared a day in advance and popped into the fridge until required. The flavours of the vinaigrette and saffron infuse beautifully with the fish. Ideally, serve this with good-quality bread or boiled and peeled new potatoes to counteract the acidity of the fish, then offer a fresh salad to provide a little crunch. A great dish to share.

½ teaspoon coriander seeds
¼ teaspoon fennel seeds
100 ml extra virgin olive oil
2 small golden shallots, thinly sliced
1 carrot, sliced
2 pinches of saffron threads
4 star anise
1½ tablespoons champagne vinegar
1½ tablespoons dry white wine
½ cup (125 ml) freshly squeezed orange juice
sea salt flakes
2 tablespoons olive oil
4 × 120 g mackerel fillets, skin-on and pin-boned
small handful of coriander leaves

1 Lightly crush the coriander and fennel seeds with a mortar and pestle and set aside.

2 Heat a small saucepan over low heat, then add 30 ml of the extra virgin olive oil. Cook the shallot and carrot for 2 minutes; do not allow to colour. Add the coriander seeds, fennel seeds, saffron and star anise and cook for a further 30 seconds. Pour in the vinegar and reduce by half. Add the white wine and reduce by half, then add the orange juice and remove from the heat. Add ½ teaspoon salt and the remaining extra virgin olive oil, then stir and set aside.

3 Heat a non-stick frying pan over medium heat and add the olive oil. Season the fish lightly with salt and pan-fry, skin-side down, for 2–3 minutes. Flip the fish over and cook for a further 2 minutes, then remove from the pan. Transfer the fish to a deep platter. Cover the fish with the fragrant vinegar mixture, scatter with the coriander leaves and leave to stand for at least 10–15 minutes to allow the flavours to develop. Serve at once.

Scotch eggs with salad cream

I know it's silly, but every time I visit the United Kingdom I make a quick trip to the deli to get my fill of all those British culinary cliches – including, of course, scotch eggs. Homemade scotch eggs are the best, and they make a fab addition to any picnic or party.

sea salt flakes
ice cubes
10 small eggs, at room temperature
500 g minced pork and veal (or 250 g each minced pork and minced veal)
2 tablespoons finely chopped flat-leaf parsley
1 teaspoon dried oregano
70 g fresh breadcrumbs
freshly ground white pepper
1 litre vegetable oil, for deep-frying
1 cup (70 g) panko breadcrumbs (see page 140)
⅓ cup (50 g) plain flour

SALAD CREAM
1½ tablespoons plain flour
1 tablespoon caster sugar
1 teaspoon mustard powder
¼ teaspoon ground turmeric
sea salt flakes and freshly ground white pepper
1 free-range egg yolk
⅓ cup (80 ml) thickened cream
¼ cup (60 ml) white vinegar, or to taste
1 tablespoon olive oil

1 Bring a saucepan of water to the boil over high heat, then add a good pinch of salt. Place a bowl of iced water next to the stove. Gently lower 8 of the eggs into the boiling water, reduce the heat to medium and simmer for 3 minutes. Remove immediately with a slotted spoon and immerse in the iced water. Remove the eggs and carefully peel off the shells. Drain and pat dry on paper towel.

2 Mix the minced pork and veal in a large bowl with the parsley, oregano, breadcrumbs, salt, pepper and 1 raw egg until nice and sticky. Dust each cooked egg lightly in flour and mould one-eighth of the mixture around each egg to form a 5 mm-thick layer. Put the coated eggs in the fridge for 20 minutes.

3 To make the salad cream, mix the flour, sugar, mustard and turmeric. Season well with salt and a pinch of pepper. In a separate bowl, mix together the egg yolk, cream and vinegar. Pour the cream mixture over the flour mixture and whisk until smooth. Whisk in the olive oil until combined. Transfer the mixture to a small saucepan and cook over medium heat, whisking constantly for 3–5 minutes or until thickened. Remove from the stove and set aside until cold. (Makes about 200 ml. Store any leftover salad cream in an airtight container in the fridge for up to 7 days.)

4 Heat the vegetable oil in a deep-fryer or heavy-based saucepan to 170°C (or until a cube of bread browns in 20 seconds).

5 Place the panko breadcrumbs in a bowl, the flour in a second bowl and the remaining raw egg in a third bowl, then whisk it with a splash of water. Add a pinch of salt and a few grinds of pepper to both the egg and flour.

6 Roll the scotch eggs first in the flour and pat off any excess, then drop into the egg mixture and coat well. Drain, removing any excess egg mixture, then roll in the panko breadcrumbs, coating well. Using a slotted spoon and working in batches, carefully lower the eggs into the hot oil and cook for 3–4 minutes or until golden and crisp. Drain on paper towel.

7 Best served at room temperature with the salad cream to the side.

Roasted beetroot salad with hazelnuts and watercress

Beetroot and sour cream is a marriage made in heaven – just think of borscht, the well-known Russian soup. Roasting beetroot is the best way to bring out that super-earthy sweetness you get from all root vegetables. This salad is a celebration of the earth and hedgerow; I have also added sweet roasted garlic, a few radishes and hazelnuts for interest and crunch, and watercress for its lovely, iron-y pepperiness.

1 red onion, quartered, root ends intact
sea salt flakes and freshly ground black pepper
4 sprigs thyme
8 cloves garlic
12 baby red beetroot, washed, stalks trimmed
    and bases scraped clean
12 baby yellow beetroot, washed, stalks trimmed
    and bases scraped clean
olive oil, for drizzling
50 g hazelnuts
100 g sour cream
4 radishes, cut into eighths
1 large handful watercress sprigs

VINAIGRETTE
1 teaspoon dijon mustard
2 tablespoons verjuice (see page 141)
1 tablespoon hazelnut oil
¼ cup (60 ml) extra virgin olive oil
sea salt flakes

1 Preheat a fan-forced oven to 180°C (200°C conventional).

2 Lay two large sheets of foil on the bench side-by-side. Place the onion on a sheet of foil, then sprinkle with a pinch of salt and a twist of pepper. Throw on 2 sprigs of thyme and 4 garlic cloves.

3 Place the beetroot on the second sheet of foil, scatter with the remaining thyme and garlic, then season with salt and pepper.

4 Drizzle the onion and beetroot with olive oil and enclose the foil around the vegetables to make two loose parcels. Transfer to a baking tray, then roast for 45 minutes or until tender. Remove the parcels from the oven and set aside to cool.

5 Peel the beetroot (ideally using disposable kitchen gloves otherwise you'll end up with stained fingers). Cut the red beetroot into quarters. Set aside.

6 Place the hazelnuts on a baking tray and roast in the oven for 4–6 minutes until the skins blister and begin to darken. Remove the hazelnuts and tip into a clean tea towel. Rub the hazelnuts with the towel to remove the skins.

7 To make the vinaigrette, whisk the mustard and verjuice in a small bowl, then add the hazelnut and olive oils in a steady stream, whisking constantly to emulsify the vinaigrette. Season with a pinch of salt. Leftover vinaigrette can be stored in an airtight container in the fridge for up to 14 days and used to dress all kinds of salads.

8 Smear the sour cream onto a platter or individual plates, then top with the beetroot, onion and garlic. Sprinkle with the radish, hazelnuts and watercress, then drizzle with the vinaigrette. Serve immediately.

Egg and bacon salad with blue cheese dressing

This is my version of a Caesar salad. It has been on the menu at Fenix and now The Boathouse on and off for ten years and continues to sell like hotcakes. Not that I dislike a nice Caesar, but it just doesn't do it for me. I personally think it needs bacon, and lots of fat, for it to taste gorgeous. The blue cheese dressing is the kicker for me – use a great blue cheese like gorgonzola piccante or stilton. Store leftover dressing, closely covered with plastic film, in the fridge for up to 3 days.

4 rashers bacon, rind removed, finely chopped
4 slices dense sourdough bread, cut into 5 mm dice
50 ml extra virgin olive oil
2 free-range eggs
3 baby cos lettuces, outer leaves discarded, halved lengthways
100 g blue cheese, such as gorgonzola piccante, crumbled
sea salt flakes and freshly ground white pepper

BLUE CHEESE DRESSING

1 quantity Basic Mayonnaise (see page 136)
100 g gorgonzola piccante, crumbled
juice of 1 lemon
sea salt and freshly ground black pepper

1 Preheat a fan-forced oven to 160°C (180°C conventional).

2 Place the bacon on a baking tray lined with baking paper, and cook for 10 minutes or until golden and crisp. Set aside.

3 Drizzle the bread with olive oil, then place on the baking tray and toast in the oven for 7 minutes or until crisp and golden. Set aside.

4 Boil the eggs in a pan of simmering water for 8 minutes. Remove with a slotted spoon and cool under cold running water. Remove the shells. Dry the eggs with paper towel and chop roughly. Set aside.

5 To make the dressing, blend the mayonnaise and gorgonzola in a blender until combined. Add the lemon juice and blend until just combined. Season to taste with salt and pepper. Set aside 200 ml of the dressing and store the rest in the fridge. (Makes 750 ml.)

6 Spoon a little dressing over a serving plate or platter and place the lettuce on top. Spoon a little more dressing over the lettuce, then scatter with the egg, bread, blue cheese and bacon. Season with salt and pepper and serve.

Summer salad of peas, baby lettuce, feta and spearmint

When I was growing up, a salad meant soft butterhead lettuce, cucumber and tomatoes – nothing wrong with that, but have a look at this recipe. Celebrate all the different leaves, soft herbs and lettuces you can buy. Make a simple, slightly sweet dressing, and voila! Oh, and maybe serve it with a Campari and soda with a little ice and a dash of orange juice for a perfect summer starter.

120 g fresh or frozen peas
ice cubes
8 thin slices flat pancetta
1 baby cos lettuce, damaged outer leaves
    discarded, inner leaves washed and dried
1 small green oak lettuce, damaged outer leaves
    discarded, inner leaves washed and dried
1 large handful unsprayed edible flowers, such as
    marigold, violets, nasturtium, wattle, lavender,
    rosemary and garlic or mixed soft herbs,
    such as dill, tarragon and perilla
handful of spearmint leaves
1 small handful of nasturtium leaves (optional)
120 g feta

LEMON VINAIGRETTE
1 teaspoon dijon mustard
1 teaspoon honey
finely grated zest and juice of 1 lemon
sea salt flakes and freshly ground black pepper
½ cup (125 ml) extra virgin olive oil

1 Preheat a fan-forced oven to 160°C (180°C conventional).

2 To make the lemon vinaigrette, whisk the mustard, honey, lemon zest and juice in a bowl. Add a pinch of salt and pepper and whisk. Drizzle in the olive oil, whisking continuously until emulsified. Set aside.

3 If using fresh peas, place in a small saucepan of boiling salted water and simmer over high heat for 2 minutes or until just tender. Drain and refresh in iced water or under cold running water until the peas are cold. Drain well on paper towel and set aside. If using frozen peas, thaw and drain on paper towel.

4 Line a baking tray with baking paper and lay the pancetta on the tray. Cover with another piece of baking paper and lay another baking tray on top to keep the pancetta flat. Bake the pancetta for 10 minutes or until it is crisp and golden. Set aside to cool. Break the pancetta into bite-sized pieces.

5 Place the lettuce, flowers, herbs and nasturtium leaves (if using) in a bowl and toss together gently. Place half of the peas and feta in a wide-based bowl, then drizzle with a generous amount of the lemon vinaigrette and season with a little salt and pepper. Place half of the lettuce leaves and flowers on top and interweave with the crisp pancetta, then scatter with a few more peas, drizzle with dressing and repeat until all the leaves, flowers, peas, feta, pancetta and vinaigrette are used.

6 Serve immediately.

Roasted red capsicum with ashed goat's cheese and basil

Pick bright long red capsicums with a nice aroma for this stunning starter. There are many beautiful Australian goats' cheeses, some soft, some aged, some coated with ash. For this recipe, choose an ashed goat's cheese.

4 long red capsicums (peppers)
⅓ cup (80 ml) extra virgin olive oil
1 clove garlic, peeled and thinly sliced
2 sprigs thyme
2 fresh bay leaves
sea salt flakes and freshly ground black pepper
200 g ashed goat's cheese, cut evenly into 6 slices
baby basil (or small basil leaves) and lemon
    wedges, to serve

1 Preheat a fan-forced oven to 180°C (200°C conventional).

2 Place the capsicums on a sheet of foil on a baking tray and drizzle on the olive oil. Scatter the garlic, thyme and bay leaves over the capsicums, then season with salt and pepper. Draw up the sides of foil to enclose, then place in the oven for 10 minutes or until the capsicums begin to char and soften slightly. Remove and leave to cool for 10 minutes. Cut the capsicums in half, then discard the seeds, if desired, but leave the stems on. Pour over the roasting juices and set aside.

3 Place the capsicum on a serving plate and top with the goat's cheese. Drizzle with the reserved roasting juices and scatter with basil, then serve with lemon wedges.

Asparagus with goat's curd and green olive tapenade SERVES 2

The candied walnuts add a lovely earthiness and sweet crunch here; little surprises that make this the perfect warm-weather salad. White anchovy fillets are anchovy fillets that have been marinated in vinegar.

table salt
1 bunch green asparagus
1 bunch white asparagus
ice cubes
1 teaspoon honey
1 teaspoon dijon mustard
finely grated zest and juice of 1 lemon
¼ cup (60 ml) extra virgin olive oil
sea salt flakes and freshly ground black pepper
1 small clove garlic, peeled and halved
1 small ficelle baguette or 2 dinner rolls,
    sliced into 2 mm-thick ovals
50 g caster sugar, plus extra for sprinkling
25 ml hot water
50 g walnuts
⅓ cup (65 g) soft fresh goat's curd
handful of baby basil sprigs
nasturtium leaves (optional), to serve

GREEN OLIVE TAPENADE
140 g pitted green olives
2 teaspoons salted capers, rinsed
2 white anchovy fillets
2 tablespoons extra virgin olive oil

1 To make the green olive tapenade, place the olives, capers, anchovies and olive oil in a food processor and blend until smooth. (Makes 125 ml. Leftover tapenade can be stored in an airtight container in the fridge for up to 7 days.)

2 Bring a large saucepan of water to the boil with a good pinch of salt.

3 Preheat a fan-forced oven to 180°C (200°C conventional).

4 Trim the asparagus by removing the woody ends (usually approximately 2 cm). Use the tip of a small knife to remove the little spurs up towards the head of the asparagus. Place a handful of ice in a bowl and cover with 1 cup (250 ml) water to refresh the asparagus, then set aside. Place the green and white asparagus in the pan of boiling salted water and cook for 2 minutes or until just tender. Carefully remove with a slotted spoon and transfer to the iced water. Leave to cool thoroughly, then remove from the iced water, drain and set aside on paper towel.

5 Mix the honey and mustard in a small bowl, then add the lemon zest and juice. Mix well and slowly whisk in 40 ml of the extra virgin olive oil, adding it one drop at a time. Add a pinch of salt and a twist of pepper and set aside.

6 Rub the garlic clove onto the sliced bread and place on a baking tray, then drizzle or brush with the remaining olive oil. Bake for 4–5 minutes or until light-golden brown. Remove from the oven and set aside.

7 Mix the sugar and hot water in a bowl to form a thick paste. Place the walnuts in the sugar mixture and stir to coat evenly, then drain. Place the drained walnuts on a baking tray lined with baking paper, then sprinkle with extra sugar. Bake for 10 minutes, stirring or moving around once or twice; they should become shiny and sugary. Remove from the oven and leave to cool.

8 Cut the asparagus into 4 cm lengths, reserving the tips, then toss with a little of the honey mustard vinaigrette.

9 To serve, spread the tapenade liberally onto a serving plate or dish and top with the asparagus. Spread the goat's curd on the toasted bread and arrange around the asparagus. Sprinkle with the candied walnuts and drizzle with a little of the vinaigrette. Toss the baby basil with a little vinaigrette and scatter carefully on top of the asparagus salad, then add nasturtium leaves, if using.

10 Serve immediately.

Confit of tomatoes

I learnt this recipe many years ago from someone who worked for the famous French chef Joël Robuchon. At the time I thought, 'What a lovely, simple way to treat such an emotive ingredient'. The coriander adds a subtle background flavour and spice to fresh ripe tomatoes. Served with grilled fish, chicken or roast lamb, these are gorgeous, or simpler still, just slice or crush onto grilled sourdough bread – mmm!

1 teaspoon white peppercorns
2 tablespoons fennel seeds
2 tablespoons coriander seeds
1 teaspoon sea salt flakes
3 cloves garlic, peeled and bruised
4 star anise
1 kg mixed heirloom tomatoes, such as black russians, yellow plum or vine-ripened, halved widthways (optional)
handful of basil sprigs
400 ml extra virgin olive oil

1 Preheat a fan-forced oven to 100°C (120°C conventional).

2 Select a baking dish or roasting pan that is large enough to hold the tomatoes in one layer (mine is 50 cm × 30 cm × 24 cm). Lightly crush the peppercorns, fennel seeds and coriander seeds with a mortar and pestle, then sprinkle over the base of the pan. Scatter on the salt and garlic, then add the star anise and evenly spread the mixture over the base of the pan. Place the tomatoes cut-side down (if halved) on top of the spices. Roughly tear the basil sprigs over the tomatoes, then place the basil stalks in between the tomatoes and flood with the olive oil.

3 Roast the tomatoes for 1 hour. Remove from the oven and leave to cool, then cover and refrigerate.

4 You can serve these straight away or store them in the fridge for up to 1 week. The tomatoes will continue to absorb the beautiful flavours of the other ingredients during this time.

Stir-fried snake beans and gai lan

I am not a big fan of the pedestrian stir-fry, which always seems to contain baby corn, carrot and capsicum. But give me snake beans and gai lan, my favourite Asian greens, and it is a different story. To my mind, Chinese sausage and crisp garlic make everything taste great, so put them all together and you can't go wrong.

1½ tablespoons peanut oil
5 cloves garlic, peeled and finely chopped
1 handful snake beans, trimmed,
    cut into 8 cm lengths
1 bunch gai lan (Chinese broccoli), damaged outer
    leaves removed, stalks trimmed and
    thinly sliced
½ teaspoon chilli flakes
2 Chinese sausages (lap cheong, see page 139),
    thinly sliced
4 tinned water chestnuts, drained, sliced
2 tablespoons light soy sauce
2 tablespoons oyster sauce
large handful of bean sprouts,
    straggly ends removed
small handful of garlic chives
small handful of coriander sprigs
steamed rice (optional), to serve

1 Heat the oil in a wok over medium heat, then add three-quarters of the garlic and stir for 2 minutes or until golden and crisp. Drain the garlic into a sieve placed over a bowl, then place the garlic on paper towel to drain further and reserve the oil.

2 Wipe out the wok, return the oil to it and place over medium heat. Stir-fry the snake beans and gai lan gently for 3–4 minutes or until they begin to soften. Add the remaining garlic, chilli flakes and sausage to the wok, then increase the heat to high to crisp the sausage a little and release the flavour from the garlic. Add the water chestnuts, soy sauce and oyster sauce, then remove from the heat.

3 Tip onto a plate, then scatter with the bean sprouts, garlic chives, coriander and crisp garlic. Serve immediately, with rice, if desired.

Sweet and sour onions

Onions are super-sweet when caramelised; adding a little hit of vinegar makes them irresistible. They work perfectly as an accompaniment to offal such as calves' or lambs' liver and gamey meats such as venison or even kangaroo. I also like to serve them alongside grilled or roast chicken or meaty fish such as blue eye trevalla and monkfish.

1½ tablespoons olive oil
20 baby onions, peeled, root ends intact
sea salt flakes and freshly ground white pepper
60 g caster sugar
100 ml sweet aged red-wine vinegar
25 g unsalted butter
50 ml water
4 sprigs thyme, plus extra (optional), to serve
2 fresh bay leaves

1 Preheat a fan-forced oven to 180°C (200°C conventional).

2 Place a shallow, heavy-based, ovenproof frying pan or enamelled cast-iron casserole over medium heat and add the olive oil and onions. Cook, stirring occasionally, for 4–5 minutes or until the onions are golden brown all over. Season with 1 teaspoon sea salt and a little pepper. Remove the onions from the pan and set aside.

3 Wipe the pan clean and return it to medium heat. Add the sugar and melt for 4 minutes or until golden. Pour in the vinegar and stir once or twice until the sugar dissolves. Simmer for 10 minutes or until reduced by two-thirds. Add the butter and water, then bring to the boil. Add the onions, thyme and bay leaves to the pan and stir gently, coating the onions in the syrup.

4 Transfer the pan to the oven and roast for 20 minutes, stirring once during this time, or until the onions are tender and you can press the tip of a small knife into them with no resistance.

5 Scatter with extra thyme sprigs, if desired, and serve.

Pesto

Although this is one of the simplest sauces to make, it packs a huge punch. Pesto taught non-Italians that pasta was not just for bolognese sauce. Brilliant with fish, tossed with pasta or stirred through sauces, the list of uses for pesto goes on and on, as do the variations. Basil is one of my favourite herbs. We receive boxes of fresh basil in my restaurant kitchen every day. Its sweet, heady smell permeates every inch of the place, reminding me how a single beautiful ingredient can be sublime.

⅓ cup (50 g) pine nuts
2 cups (500 ml) water
ice cubes
1 bunch basil, leaves picked
½ clove garlic, peeled
sea salt flakes
⅔ cup (160 ml) extra virgin olive oil
30 g parmesan, grated

1 Preheat the oven to 160°C fan-forced (180°C conventional).

2 Roast the pine nuts on a baking tray for 4 minutes or until light-golden brown. Set aside.

3 Bring the water to the boil in a saucepan. Have a bowl filled with a handful of ice and the water next to the stove. Set aside.

4 Plunge the basil leaves in the boiling water for 30–40 seconds, then drain and immerse immediately in the iced water. Drain the basil, squeeze dry and shred.

5 Place the garlic and 1 teaspoon of salt in a mortar and pound with the pestle to form a paste. Add the pine nuts and pound into a meal. Add the basil and pound for 2 minutes to produce a coarse paste, slowly drizzling in the olive oil and pounding to incorporate. Stir in the parmesan.

6 Pesto is best served fresh, but can be stored in the fridge in an airtight container under a thin layer of oil to prevent the surface from oxidising for up to 2 days.

MAINS

Roasted beef sirloin with Yorkshire puddings

I have included this recipe as it gives me an excuse to make these super-light Yorkshire puddings again. Yorkshire pudding batter is best made the night before and stored in the fridge.

sea salt flakes and freshly ground white pepper
1 tablespoon thyme leaves
50 ml olive oil
1 × 1.5 kg piece beef sirloin, tied with kitchen string, brought to room temperature
5 small golden shallots, peeled
2 cloves garlic, peeled
2 fresh bay leaves
1 tablespoon plain flour
splash of dry white wine
100 ml Beef Stock (see page 134)

YORKSHIRE PUDDINGS
130 g plain flour, sifted
3 free-range eggs
350 ml milk
sea salt flakes
¾ cup (180 ml) melted lard or vegetable oil

1 To make the Yorkshire pudding batter, tip the flour into a mixing bowl and make a well in the centre. Break the eggs into the centre and add half of the milk and 1 teaspoon salt. Whisk to form a batter, starting from the centre of the well and working outwards to incorporate the flour. Whisk the remaining milk into the mixture until the batter is smooth, then cover with plastic film. Rest the batter in the fridge overnight, if you have time, or for at least 30 minutes.

2 Preheat the oven to 180°C fan-forced (200°C conventional).

3 Rub 2 tablespoons salt, 3 tablespoons pepper, thyme and 1 tablespoon of the olive oil over the entire surface of the beef. Heat the remaining olive oil in a heavy-based flameproof roasting pan over high heat and fry each side of the beef for 4–5 minutes, turning until golden brown all over.

Add the shallots, garlic and bay leaves to the pan, then transfer to the oven and roast the beef for 45 minutes, basting regularly with the juices.

4 Remove the beef from the oven, remove the string, cover with foil and rest for 10–15 minutes. Meanwhile, increase the oven temperature to 220°C fan-forced (240°C conventional).

5 To cook the Yorkshire puddings, place a heavy-based non-stick muffin pan on a baking tray and heat in the oven for 5 minutes. Fill each muffin mould one-third full with melted lard or vegetable oil (approximately 1 cm deep). Return the baking tray with the muffin pan to the oven for a few minutes to heat, then carefully slide the muffin pan from the oven and evenly divide the batter among the moulds, filling them to just below the top. Carefully return the muffin pan to the oven. Cook the Yorkshire puddings for 12 minutes or until golden. Carefully remove the tray from the oven and flip each pudding over in the moulds to expose the bottom, then return to the oven to colour and firm up for approximately 3 minutes. Remove and turn out the yorkies.

6 Meanwhile, place the roasting pan of cooking juices over medium heat, discard the bay leaves, then crush the garlic and shallots into the juices with the back of a fork. Add the flour and stir it into the juices with a wooden spoon, then cook for 1 minute or until the sauce thickens. Add the white wine and stir to combine, then add the stock a little at a time, stirring continuously. Bring to the boil and simmer for 2 minutes, then pour into a gravy jug.

7 Slice the beef and serve with the gravy and Yorkshire puddings.

The perfect sirloin steak with capsicum butter

Cooking steak perfectly every time is not easy, so increasing the chances of achieving a predictable outcome is the name of the game. That means buying steaks that are the same size and thickness, then preheating the grillplate to the same temperature each time you barbecue. Timing is also crucial, so follow the guidelines below. If you stick to these simple rules, it will eliminate the guesswork and, with a little practice, you'll have perfectly cooked steak every time.

4 thick sirloin steaks (about 300 g each),
    brought to room temperature
sea salt flakes and freshly ground white pepper
2 tablespoons olive oil
2 tablespoons extra virgin olive oil
handful of thyme leaves
1 stem rosemary, leaves chopped, plus extra leaves
    (optional), to serve

CAPSICUM BUTTER
2 small red capsicums (peppers)
2 cloves garlic, peeled
1 anchovy fillet
½ teaspoon smoked paprika (see page 140)
sea salt flakes and freshly ground white pepper
150 g unsalted butter, chopped and softened

1 To make the capsicum butter, char the capsicums directly over a gas flame or on a hot barbecue grillplate. As the skins blacken and blister, turn and cook until blackened on all sides. Transfer to a bowl, then cover with plastic film. Leave in a warm spot for 20 minutes or until cool enough to handle. Drain the capsicums on paper towel, then peel off the skin with your fingers (it should come away easily). Cut the capsicums in half and remove and discard the seeds and stems. Blend the capsicum, garlic, anchovy, paprika, salt and a few grinds of pepper in a food processor until a puree forms. Add the butter and blend until fully combined, smooth and red. Using a flexible spatula (see page 140), transfer the butter to a bowl, then cover with plastic film and set aside.

2 Preheat the barbecue grillplate on high for 5 minutes then turn down to medium heat. Lightly season the steaks with salt and pepper and drizzle with olive oil.

3 Place the steaks on the grill, starting at the top left-hand corner of the grill and laying them at a 45-degree angle. Working towards the right-hand side, lay the remaining steaks in a row next to each other. (This means you are working across and down the grill to create a crisscross grill mark on each side of the steaks.) Grill the steaks at this angle for half of the cooking time for one side (see below), then turn the steaks around in the opposite direction at 45 degrees and cook for the remaining half of the cooking time. Turn over and repeat on the other side.
- For rare: 2 minutes on each side.
- For medium–rare: 4 minutes on each side.
- For medium: 5 minutes on each side
- For well-done: 8 minutes on each side.

4 Remove the steaks and place on a plate to rest for half of their cooking time. Place the extra virgin olive oil in a small bowl and stir through the thyme and rosemary. Brush this herb oil onto the steaks while they are resting, then season with salt.

5 Serve the steaks topped with a spoonful of capsicum butter, and scattered with extra rosemary leaves (if using).

Red braised beef and daikon

The pleasure of this dish lies in the lovely stock, so make sure there's plenty of it to go around – you may like to serve this as more of a steaming hot wet dish. Bean and chilli sauce or paste is made from fermented soy beans and chillies, and is available from Asian food stores.

20 g dried shiitake mushrooms, soaked in
    hot water for 45 minutes
¼ cup (60 ml) peanut oil
800 g short beef ribs, cut into sections
    between the bones
2 tablespoons bean and chilli sauce
5 cm piece ginger, sliced
10 cloves garlic, peeled
1 teaspoon Sichuan pepper
1 long red chilli, finely chopped
100 g yellow rock sugar (see page 141)
2 litres Chicken Stock (see page 134)
½ cup (125 ml) light soy sauce
½ cup (125 ml) dark soy sauce
1½ cups (375 ml) Chinese rice wine
3 pieces dried mandarin or tangerine peel
5 sticks cinnamon
8 star anise
1 daikon, cut into 3 cm-thick pieces
1 onion, cut into 8 wedges
8 spring onions, cut into 2 cm lengths
1 teaspoon sesame oil
coriander leaves and steamed rice (optional),
    to serve

1 Drain the mushrooms, reserving the strained soaking liquid, then remove and discard the woody stalks.

2 Heat a heavy-based saucepan or enamelled cast-iron casserole over high heat and add the peanut oil. Add the beef in batches and cook until browned on all sides and nicely caramelised. Reduce the heat to low, then discard any excess oil. Return all the beef to the pan. Add the bean and chilli sauce and cook for 1 minute, then add the ginger, garlic, Sichuan pepper, chilli, rock sugar, stock, soy sauces, rice wine, citrus peel, cinnamon and star anise.

3 Bring to the boil over high heat, then reduce the heat to low. Add the mushrooms, reserved soaking liquid, daikon and onion, then pop on a lid and simmer for 2 hours or until the beef is soft and tender. Add the spring onion and sesame oil, then scatter with coriander and serve with steamed rice, if desired.

Beef, onion and Guinness pies

These tasty little pies remind me of the steak and kidney pies Mum used to make when we were kids – they were Dad's favourite. There is enough filling to make twenty pies, so freeze the leftover and use it the next time you want to make a batch, or serve it with mashed potato for a hearty dinner.

2 litres Beef Stock (see page 134)
1.5 kg trimmed chuck steak, cut into 4 cm pieces
sea salt flakes and freshly ground white pepper
⅓ cup (80 ml) olive oil, plus extra for greasing
1 carrot, cut into large chunks
5 onions, sliced
1 head garlic, cloves separated, peeled and chopped
4 sprigs thyme
2 tablespoons plain flour
2 fresh bay leaves
1 × 440 ml can Guinness
1 free-range egg, beaten
tomato sauce (optional), to serve

MAGGIE BEER'S SOUR-CREAM PASTRY
200 g chilled unsalted butter, chopped
1⅔ cups (250 g) plain flour, plus extra for dusting
½ cup (125 ml) sour cream

1 Place the beef stock in a heavy-based saucepan and simmer over medium–high heat for 1 hour or until reduced by half. Set aside.

2 Season the beef generously with salt and pepper. Heat 60 ml of the olive oil in an enamelled cast-iron casserole over high heat, then cook the beef in two batches until well browned on all sides. Remove from the pan and set aside. Add the carrot and cook for 5–6 minutes or until golden. Remove from the pan and set aside.

3 Add the remaining olive oil to the pan, then add the onion, garlic and thyme and cook over low heat (use a simmer mat, see page 140, if necessary) for 40 minutes or until the onion is soft and translucent, stirring occasionally. Increase the heat to medium–high and cook for a further 3 minutes or so. Add the flour and continue to cook for 3–4 minutes.

4 Preheat the oven to 145°C fan-forced (165°C conventional).

5 Return the beef and carrot to the pan, then add the bay leaves and Guinness. Bring to the boil over high heat, then add the reduced beef stock and return to the boil. Place a lid on top immediately, then transfer to the oven and cook for about 2 hours. Remove from the oven and leave to cool. Remove the chunks of beef and carrot and chop them into 1 cm pieces, then return them to the onion gravy. Refrigerate until cold.

6 Meanwhile, to make the sour-cream pastry, place the butter and flour in the bowl of an electric mixer or food processor, then blend until the mixture resembles large breadcrumbs. Gradually add the sour cream, mixing until the pastry just comes together. Turn onto a bench dusted with 1 tablespoon flour, then bring together with your hands. Shape into a disc, then wrap in plastic film and chill for at least 20 minutes.

7 Increase the oven temperature to 180°C fan-forced (200°C conventional). Grease 10 holes of a 12-hole muffin pan with a little olive oil.

8 Roll out the pastry to 3 mm thick, using a little extra flour for dusting. Cut out ten 9.5 cm rounds for the pie bases and ten 6.5 cm rounds for the pie lids. Place a 9.5 cm pastry round in each hole, then press it in lightly with your fingers, so that the pastry is 1 cm above the mould. Fill each hole with some of the beef mixture, then top with a 6.5 cm pastry round and crimp the edges to seal in the filling.

9 Brush the pastry tops with beaten egg and bake for 25 minutes or until golden. Remove from the oven and leave to stand for 5 minutes. Turn out and serve with tomato sauce, if desired.

Roast chicken with fondant potato, minted peas and spinach

For best results buy a good-quality, corn-fed, free-range chicken, remove the wishbone to make it easier to carve and truss it to help it hold its form. The flavour of the pan juices is far superior to those from an everyday chicken.

1 × 1.6 kg free-range chicken
1 lemon, quartered
2 sprigs thyme
2 cloves garlic, peeled
table salt
1½ tablespoons olive oil
5 small golden shallots, peeled
splash of dry white wine
100 ml Chicken Stock (see page 134)

FONDANT POTATO
170 g unsalted butter, chopped
4 large desiree potatoes, cut into 7 cm ×
**   5 cm × 1 cm-thick rectangles**
4 sprigs thyme
100 ml water
sea salt flakes

MINTED PEAS AND SPINACH
½ cup (125 ml) olive oil
1 small clove garlic, thinly sliced
240 g fresh or frozen peas
2 handfuls spinach
16 mint leaves, chopped

1 Preheat a fan-forced oven to 180°C (200°C conventional).

2 To remove the wishbone from the chicken, lift the neck skin to reveal the breast. Scrape the point of a small sharp knife down the wishbone (it looks like an upside-down 'V' shape). Put your fingers behind the bone and tug to remove it. Stuff the cavity with the lemon, thyme and 1 clove of the garlic. Truss the chicken with kitchen twine.

3 Heat a flameproof roasting pan over high heat. Season the chicken with salt and pour the olive oil into the pan. Brown the chicken lightly on all sides, starting with one leg, turning it over to brown the other leg, then the breast. Turn the chicken onto its back, then roast for 20 minutes.

4 Baste the chicken with the pan juices. Add the shallots and remaining garlic and roast for a further 40 minutes or until the chicken is cooked. To test, pierce the thigh at the thickest part – the juices should run clear. Transfer the chicken to a large plate and rest for 10 minutes.

5 Meanwhile, to make the fondant potato, melt the butter in a deep heavy-based frying pan over medium heat. As the butter begins to bubble, add the potato and thyme in layers. Reduce the heat to low, then cook for 10 minutes or until the potato is golden. Turn the potato over and cook for another 10 minutes or until golden. Add the water; the butter will foam and darken slightly. Baste the potato well and continue to cook for another 10 minutes or until tender. Remove from the heat, then leave to stand for 5 minutes. Season with salt. Set aside and keep warm.

6 Place the roasting pan of cooking juices over low heat, then crush the roasted garlic and shallots into the pan with the back of a fork. Add the wine and stock and simmer over low heat for 2 minutes. Set aside.

7 To make the minted peas and spinach, warm the olive oil in a saucepan over low heat, then add the garlic and leave to infuse for 30 seconds. Add the peas and increase the heat to medium, then cook for 2 minutes or until they are warmed through. Add the spinach and mint, then remove from the heat and stir, allowing the spinach to wilt.

8 Cut the chicken into quarters and serve with the fondant potato, gravy and minted peas and spinach.

Chicken and verjuice fricassee

I have a photograph from my college days, taken when I might have just been pushing seventeen, knife in hand, wearing a tall starched hat and cutting a chicken for 'saute'. One of the first things I ever learnt when I started training to be a chef was how to neatly divide a bird into eight pieces (or ten, if you count the winglets). It's the first step for a thousand different dishes, including this lovely fricassee. I still enjoy cutting up a chicken with the same knife – without the starched hat now, of course.

¼ cup (60 ml) olive oil, plus extra if needed
2 onions, sliced
5 cloves garlic, peeled and sliced
2 fresh bay leaves
sea salt flakes
4 sprigs thyme, leaves picked
1 × 1.4 kg free-range chicken
½ cup (125 ml) verjuice (see page 141)
200 ml Chicken Stock (see page 134)
freshly ground white pepper
4 king brown mushrooms, thickly sliced
thyme sprigs (optional), to serve

1 Heat 1½ tablespoons of the olive oil in a heavy-based saucepan over medium heat, then add the onion, garlic and bay leaves. Fry for 5 minutes or until golden, stirring regularly, then add a good pinch of salt and the thyme. Reduce the heat to low–medium and cook for 25 minutes or until the onion is soft, sweet and golden.

2 Meanwhile remove the legs from the chicken, then divide at the joint into thighs and drumsticks. Remove the breasts from the carcass and divide each breast into 2 pieces. (Reserve the carcass for making the Chicken stock on page 134, if desired.)

3 Add the verjuice to the pan with the onion and stir well, scraping off any sediment on the base of the pan to add to the flavour. Simmer the verjuice over low–medium heat for 4–5 minutes or until reduced by half. Add the chicken stock, then bring to the boil to allow the flavours to combine. Set aside.

4 Heat a heavy-based non-stick or enamelled cast-iron frying pan with a tight-fitting lid over high heat. Add the remaining olive oil, then gently add the chicken leg pieces. Cook for 8 minutes, turning frequently, then add the breast pieces and continue to cook for another 8 minutes, turning frequently. Season the chicken with salt and pepper and transfer to a plate. Add a dash more oil to the pan if required, then fry the mushrooms for 4 minutes until golden on all sides. Remove from the pan and set aside with the chicken.

5 Tip the onion mixture into the pan and use a wooden spoon to scrape the sediment from the base of the pan. Return the chicken and mushrooms to the pan. Put the lid on and simmer for 3 minutes to reheat and ensure the chicken is cooked through.

6 Scatter with thyme sprigs (if using). Serve immediately.

Coq au vin

Coq au vin is an all-time classic that is hard to beat – not only is it rich and warming but it is packed with flavour. There is no way around it: you need more than a good slosh of red wine to make this dish something really special. If you feel that's too extravagant, then by all means be a little more frugal with the wine and port; it's up to you. You will need to marinate the chicken the day before you wish to serve it.

You can substitute chicken maryland pieces but I recommend using a whole chicken as it is more economical.

1 × 1.4 kg free-range chicken
400 ml red wine
150 ml ruby port
2 cloves garlic, peeled
20 golden shallots, peeled
1 × 300 g piece bacon, rind removed,
    cut into 1.5 cm pieces
3 sprigs thyme
1 fresh bay leaf
2 tablespoons olive oil
16 button mushrooms, stalks trimmed
table salt and freshly ground white pepper
200 ml Veal Stock (see page 134)
400 ml Chicken Stock (see page 134)
1½ tablespoons cornflour
1 teaspoon water
crusty bread, to serve

1 Cut the chicken into 8 pieces. First, remove the legs from the chicken, then divide at the joint into thighs and drumsticks. Remove the breasts from the carcass and divide each breast into 2 pieces. (Reserve the carcass for making the Chicken stock on page 134, if desired.) Place the chicken, wine and port in a large non-reactive dish, then add the garlic, shallots, bacon, thyme and bay leaf. Cover and refrigerate for 24 hours.

2 Drain the chicken, garlic, shallots and bacon well, reserving the marinade. Pat the chicken dry with paper towel if necessary.

3 Heat the oil in a flameproof casserole or large heavy-based saucepan over high heat, then add the bacon from the marinade and cook until a light-golden brown. Remove and set aside. Cook the shallots from the marinade for 2–3 minutes or until a light-golden brown, then remove and set aside. Add the mushrooms to the pan and cook for 2–3 minutes, then remove and set aside.

4 Season the chicken with salt and pepper, then add to the pan and brown over medium heat on all sides for 4–5 minutes. Meanwhile, bring the marinade to the boil in a saucepan over high heat. Skim the surface, then strain through a fine strainer, reserving the thyme and bay leaf.

5 Return the shallots and bacon to the pan of chicken and immediately pour in the hot marinade. Return to the boil over high heat and simmer for 4–5 minutes or until the liquid has reduced by two-thirds. Add both stocks and the reserved garlic, thyme and bay leaf. Bring back to the boil and turn the heat down to low, then simmer, covered, for a further 45 minutes.

6 Remove the chicken, bacon, mushrooms and shallots from the pan and set aside. Strain the sauce through a fine strainer, reserving the bay leaf. Return the sauce to the pan and bring it back to the boil over high heat. Mix the cornflour with the water, then whisk it into the sauce. Reduce the heat to low and simmer for 5 minutes or until the sauce thickens.

7 Return the chicken, bacon, mushrooms, shallots and bay leaf to the pan and simmer for a further 5 minutes or until warmed through. Serve with crusty bread.

Vietnamese chicken coleslaw

Once tried, this Vietnamese-inspired coleslaw will become a firm favourite – it's so fresh and very more-ish. Trips to your local Asian grocer will reveal so many new ingredients, such as little packets of crispy fried garlic and shallots, different crackers and garlic chives. Buy and try – that's my motto!

Poaching is a lovely way to cook chicken. Because poaching is done at such a low temperature (around 100°C), shrinkage is minimal and the resulting meat is moist and tender. As the chicken cools in the stock it cooks completely without using further heat. The chicken effectively 'rests' in the stock as it cools, resulting in tender, juicy meat.

1 × 1 kg free-range chicken
handful of coriander leaves, well washed,
    stalks and roots reserved
2 cloves garlic, peeled
1 long red chilli, split
1 stick lemongrass, white part only,
    bruised with the back of a knife
½ small Chinese cabbage, finely shredded
1 carrot, finely shredded
½ red onion, thinly sliced
1 green mango or green pawpaw, finely shredded
small handful of Vietnamese mint leaves,
    plus extra to serve
2 large handfuls of bean sprouts
handful of deep-fried shallots (see page 139)
3 tablespoons sesame seeds
3 tablespoons fried garlic (see page 140)
coriander leaves and sesame crackers, to serve

NUOC MAM DRESSING
75 g grated palm sugar (see page 140)
100 ml water
small piece ginger, chopped
1 clove garlic, peeled
1 long red chilli
100 ml fish sauce
juice of 2 limes

1 Place the chicken in a large saucepan and cover with cold water. Add the coriander roots, garlic, chilli and lemongrass. Bring to the boil over high heat, then reduce the heat to medium and cook for 30 minutes. Turn off the heat and leave the chicken to cook completely as it cools in the stock.

2 When the chicken is cool enough to handle, remove it from the pan. Strain the stock, then transfer it to an airtight container, label and store in the fridge for up to 5 days or freezer for up to 2 months. Shred the chicken meat and discard the bones, then place meat in a large bowl and set aside.

3 For the nuoc mam dressing, place the palm sugar and 50 ml of the water in a small saucepan over medium heat, stirring to dissolve the sugar; don't let it come to the boil. Set aside to cool.

4 Blend the ginger, garlic, chilli, fish sauce and remaining water in a food processor, then stir it into the cool palm sugar syrup. Add the lime juice and set aside.

5 Add the cabbage, carrot, onion, mango or pawpaw, coriander leaves, Vietnamese mint and bean sprouts to the chicken and mix through. Spoon over a generous amount of the dressing. Keep leftover dressing in an airtight container in the fridge for up to 10 days and serve with grilled fish or chicken. Add the deep-fried shallots, sesame seeds and fried garlic.

6 Spoon the salad into bowls, then scatter with a little more coriander and Vietnamese mint and throw on some sesame crackers, then serve.

Duck confit with warm brussels sprout and bacon salad SERVES 4

Duck confit originated as a peasant dish devised to cook the toughest goose or duck, then preserve it in its own fat to see you through the long, hard winter months. The duck needs to be coated in a spiced salt mixture and refrigerated for twelve to twenty-four hours before you start cooking. However, the crisp skin of a well-cooked duck confit and the soft meat that falls apart under the pressure of an eagerly held fork is well worth this time and effort. If you wish to confit the duck in advance, it can be stored in the fridge covered in the reserved fat for up to two weeks. Rendered duck fat is now available in tins from good delis or specialty food stores.

6 white peppercorns
1 clove
½ star anise
2 tablespoons rock salt
4 duck marylands
300 ml rendered duck fat (see page 139)
2 sprigs thyme
2 fresh bay leaves

WARM BRUSSELS SPROUT AND BACON SALAD
30 g unsalted butter
4 rashers bacon, rind removed, thinly sliced
2 cloves garlic, peeled and thinly sliced
16 brussels sprouts, finely sliced
¼ cup (60 ml) red-wine vinegar
table salt and freshly ground white pepper

1 Crush the peppercorns, clove and star anise with a mortar and pestle, then mix with the rock salt. Sprinkle half of the salt mixture into a 2 litre-capacity ceramic dish. Place the duck marylands on top and sprinkle over the remaining salt mixture. Cover with plastic film and refrigerate for 12–24 hours.

2 Preheat a fan-forced oven to 140°C (160°C conventional).

3 Brush off and discard the salt mixture from the duck, then pat dry with paper towel. Lay the duck, skin-side down, in a baking dish or roasting pan and place in the oven. The fat will begin to render after 15 minutes. Top up the pan with the rendered duck fat until the duck is just covered, then add the thyme and bay leaves. Continue to cook for another 1 hour or until the duck is tender. Remove the duck and strain the fat. Leave the fat to cool, then set aside.

4 Reduce the oven temperature to 100°C (120°C conventional), then return the duck to the pan and put into the oven while you prepare the sprouts.

5 To make the salad, pour 30 ml of the reserved duck fat into a heavy-based non-stick frying pan. Add the butter and melt over medium heat. When the butter begins to bubble, fry the bacon and garlic for 3 minutes or until golden. Add the sprouts and cook for another 3–4 minutes, keeping the sprouts firm to the bite. Add the vinegar and cook for another 1 minute. Remove from the heat, then season with salt and add a few turns of pepper.

6 Serve the duck with the warm brussels sprout and bacon salad.

Lamb tagine with preserved lemon and dates

Tagines take their name from the clay pot that these North African-style stews are traditionally cooked in. The tagine is glazed and fired so, once soaked, it can be used directly over an open flame or on the stovetop and it won't crack. The conical lid is designed so that the moisture from the bubbling contents travels up its sides, then condenses and falls back into the stew, keeping it beautifully moist. I am a convert to this clever bit of age-old kit. If you are using a tagine, cook on the stovetop for the entire time. However, if you don't have one, an enamelled cast-iron casserole will do the job nicely.

2 tablespoons coriander seeds
2 tablespoons cumin seeds
1 teaspoon caraway seeds
1 bunch coriander
1 onion, cut into quarters
2 heads garlic, cloves separated and peeled
2 preserved lemon quarters
2 tablespoons olive oil
1 kg boned trimmed lamb shoulder, cut into 4 cm
    chunks (about 1.3 kg before trimming)
1 tablespoon sumac (see page 141)
2 sticks cinnamon
pinch of saffron threads
sea salt flakes
400 ml Chicken Stock (see page 134)
1 cup (160 g) blanched almonds
10 dates, pitted
couscous (optional), to serve

1 Grind the coriander, cumin and caraway seeds with a mortar and pestle. Set aside.

2 Reserve half of the coriander leaves for serving, then chop the well-washed coriander roots, stems and remaining leaves and place in a blender. Add the onion, garlic and 1 preserved lemon quarter, then blend until a smooth paste forms.

3 Place 1½ tablespoons of the olive oil in a tagine or enamelled cast-iron casserole over high heat, then fry the lamb in batches for 2–3 minutes, turning until golden brown on all sides. Reduce the heat to medium, then return all the lamb to the pan and add the ground spices and sumac. Cook for 2–3 minutes, stirring to release the aroma from the spices.

4 Preheat the oven to 155°C fan-forced (175°C conventional).

5 Spread the coriander and onion paste over the lamb, then add the cinnamon, saffron and 2 teaspoons of salt. Pour in the chicken stock and bring to the boil over medium heat, stirring to mix. Reduce the heat to low, put on the lid and transfer to the oven to cook for 2 hours. (If using a tagine, leave on the stove over very low heat – ideally with a simmer mat – with the lid on.)

6 Meanwhile, place the almonds on a baking tray, drizzle with the remaining olive oil and bake for 10 minutes or until golden, then set aside.

7 When the lamb is tender, remove the casserole from the oven or tagine from the heat and add the dates, then leave to stand for 5 minutes. Discard the flesh from the remaining preserved lemon and finely chop the rind, then stir into the pan. Remove and discard the cinnamon sticks, if desired.

8 Scatter the almonds and reserved coriander leaves over the lamb, then serve with couscous, if desired.

Gary's lamb and tomato curry

A good friend gave me this family recipe about fifteen years ago. It is a beautiful curry that is typically Sri Lankan. It was the first time I had made a curry using so many individual spices rather than a prepared curry powder. The trick is to roast small quantities of whole spices to release their flavour and then grind them each time you wish to use them.

This recipe is a starting point for making lots of different great curries. You could use chicken or beef instead of lamb (just adjust the cooking time) and other root vegetables instead of potatoes.

½ cup (125 ml) peanut oil
1 kg boneless lamb leg or shoulder,
    cut into 4 cm chunks
3 large onions, sliced
1 large piece ginger, roughly chopped
6 cloves garlic, peeled
4 long red chillies
30 ml water
3 tablespoons cumin seeds
3 tablespoons coriander seeds
1 tablespoon table salt
1 teaspoon ground turmeric
2 pieces mace
2 teaspoons chilli powder
2 tablespoons sweet paprika
6 cloves
2 sticks cinnamon
8 cardamom pods, crushed
5 star anise
150 ml white vinegar
2 tablespoons tomato paste
1 × 400 g tin chopped tomato
2 sprigs fresh curry leaves, plus extra
    to serve (optional)
1 litre Chicken Stock (see page 134)
½ bunch coriander, leaves picked and roots
    scraped and finely chopped
6 kipfler potatoes, halved on the diagonal
75 g raw cashews
steamed rice, to serve

1 Heat 90 ml of the oil in a large heavy-based saucepan or enamelled cast-iron casserole over high heat. Working in batches, brown the lamb for 6–8 minutes, stirring until it is well browned on all sides, then remove and set aside. Add the onion to the pan and cook over low heat, stirring occasionally, for 20 minutes or until golden and very soft.

2 Meanwhile, blend the ginger, garlic, chilli, water and remaining oil to a paste in a blender or food processor, then set aside.

3 Dry-roast the cumin and coriander seeds in a non-stick frying pan over medium heat until fragrant. Grind the cumin and coriander seeds with a mortar and pestle or spice grinder, then mix in the salt, turmeric, mace, chilli, paprika, cloves, cinnamon, cardamom and star anise.

4 Add the spice mixture to the onion. Mix well and cook over medium heat for 5 minutes, stirring regularly to toast the spices. Stir in the vinegar. Add the lamb and its juices and the ginger paste to the pan and stir. Add the tomato paste, tomato, curry leaves and stock. Bring to the boil, then reduce the heat to low and add the coriander root. Simmer over low heat for 1 hour. Add the potato and cook for another 1 hour, stirring regularly. Add a little water during cooking if required.

5 When the lamb is tender, dry-roast the cashews in a non-stick frying pan over medium heat for 3–4 minutes or until golden, then roughly crush. Add the cashews and coriander leaves to the pan and stir lightly, then scatter with extra curry leaves (if using). Serve the curry with steamed rice.

Braised lamb neck with fennel and olives

This dish is inspired by Angelo Sanfilippo, my chef at The Boathouse. His parents come from Foggia in the southwest of Italy, where lamb and fennel cooked with olives make a regular appearance on the family's table. This works really well accompanied by either some crusty bread, a nice dish of potatoes crushed with extra virgin olive oil or crisp-fried or wet polenta.

1½ tablespoons olive oil, plus extra for drizzling
4 lamb neck fillets
table salt and freshly ground white pepper
1 bulb fennel, sliced
1 onion, sliced
2 cloves garlic, peeled and sliced
1 sprig thyme
½ fresh bay leaf
100 ml white wine
800 ml Veal Stock (see page 134)
100 g kalamata olives, pitted
rosemary sprigs with flowers intact (optional),
   to serve
crusty bread (optional), to serve

1 Preheat a fan-forced oven to 120°C (140°C conventional).

2 Heat a heavy-based ovenproof saucepan or enamelled cast-iron casserole over high heat and add the olive oil. Season the lamb with salt and pepper and brown well for 5–6 minutes. Remove the lamb and set aside.

3 Add the fennel, onion and garlic to the pan and cook over high heat for 8 minutes or until golden. Add the thyme, bay leaf and wine and simmer until the wine has almost evaporated. Add the stock and return the lamb to the pan, then bring to the boil. Skim off any fat that has floated to the top. Cover and cook in the oven for 3 hours or until tender.

4 Remove the lamb from the pan and set aside. Reduce the sauce over high heat by half to intensify its flavour; there should be just enough sauce left to serve 4. Return the lamb to the pan and add the olives to warm through.

5 Divide the lamb among four plates, then season to taste and spoon the sauce over the lamb. Drizzle with olive oil, garnish with rosemary sprigs (if using), and serve with crusty bread, if desired.

Veal fricassee with broad beans and peas

An oldie but a goodie. The secret is to make sure the meat is cooked long enough so it is super-tender (and don't worry about the cream separating – it will be okay). To lighten the fricassee, pour the sauce into a large jug and place the veal and vegetables into serving bowls. Blitz the sauce with a stick blender until light and frothy, then pour over the veal and vegetables and serve.

1 kg boneless veal leg, cut into 3 cm pieces
3 litres water
2 tablespoons olive oil
2 onions, sliced
1 head garlic, halved widthways
2 sticks celery, thinly sliced
3 fresh bay leaves
4 sprigs thyme
6 white peppercorns
sea salt flakes
200 ml dry white wine
3 litres Chicken Stock (see page 134)
300 ml thickened cream
1 tablespoon cornflour
1 tablespoon water
12 white button mushrooms, trimmed
squeeze of lemon juice
800 g fresh broad bean pods (to yield 200 g podded beans) or 200 g frozen broad beans
500 g fresh pea pods (to yield 160 g podded peas) or 160 g frozen peas
20 g unsalted butter
tarragon leaves (optional), to serve

1 Place the veal in a large heavy-based saucepan or enamelled cast-iron casserole and cover with the water, then bring to the boil over high heat. Remove from the heat and drain in a colander, discarding the water. Rinse the veal under cold water and clean the pan. (This process removes any impurities, such as blood, from the veal, resulting in a lovely white sauce.)

2 Heat the olive oil in the cleaned and dried pan over medium heat for 1 minute. Add the onion, garlic, celery, bay leaves, thyme, peppercorns and 1 teaspoon of sea salt and cook for 2 minutes. Add the wine and simmer until the wine reduces by half. Return the veal to the pan.

3 Add the stock and increase the heat to high. Bring to the boil, then reduce the heat to low and simmer for 1–1½ hours or until the veal is tender, skimming the surface occasionally. Remove from the heat. Remove the veal from the pan and set aside. Strain the stock through a fine-mesh sieve over a bowl and discard the vegetables, herbs and spices. Clean the pan, then strain the stock again into the pan. Reduce the stock over high heat for 25 minutes or until you have 600 ml.

4 Add the cream, then bring to the boil and simmer for 3 minutes. Combine the cornflour with the water to make a paste, then add to the boiling sauce. Stir the sauce until it thickens, then simmer for 3 minutes. Return the veal to the pan, add the mushrooms, then simmer for 5 minutes over low heat. Season with a pinch of salt and lemon juice. Set aside.

5 Meanwhile, blanch the podded broad beans and peas in a pan of boiling salted water for 2 minutes, then drain well and toss with the butter.

6 Divide the veal fricassee among four bowls, then scatter with the broad beans, peas and tarragon (if using) and serve.

Braised veal shanks with lentils and salsa verde

As you probably know by now, I love a good stew. Slow cooking is the perfect way to tease out all the delicious flavours from whatever you've thrown into your pot. This technique results in beautifully braised meat that is full of flavour and super-tender – it should be just soft enough that it falls from the bone when you push your fork in. Yum!

¼ cup (60 ml) extra virgin olive oil
1 large carrot, diced
1 onion, diced
1 stick celery, diced
1 head garlic, cloves separated, peeled
　　and thinly sliced
4 small veal shanks (about 420 g each), French
　　trimmed (optional, see page 140)
2 sprigs thyme
2 fresh bay leaves
5 black peppercorns
sea salt flakes
200 ml dry white wine
1 litre Chicken Stock (see page 134),
　　plus extra if needed
200 g green Puy-style lentils

SALSA VERDE
large handful of flat-leaf parsley leaves
handful of dill leaves
½ clove garlic, peeled
finely grated zest of 1 lemon
2 tablespoons salted capers, rinsed and drained
½ cup (125 ml) extra virgin olive oil
1 × 55 g tin soft green peppercorns, drained
sea salt flakes and freshly ground white pepper

1 Preheat the oven to 165°C fan-forced (185°C conventional).

2 Heat the olive oil in an enamelled cast-iron or other casserole, then add the carrot, onion, celery and garlic and cook over medium heat for 6–8 minutes to release their aromas. Add the veal and cook for 2–3 minutes, turning to colour without browning. Add the thyme, bay leaves, peppercorns, a pinch of salt and the wine, then bring to the boil over high heat and simmer for 10 minutes or until the wine has reduced by half. Add the stock and bring to the boil. Reduce the heat to low so the braising liquid is just ticking over, then put a lid on.

3 Transfer the casserole to the oven and cook for 1½ hours or until the meat is soft and tender. Check the level of liquid every now and again and add more stock, if necessary.

4 Meanwhile, rinse the lentils in a fine-mesh sieve under cold running water. Bring a small pan of water to the boil over high heat, then add the lentils, reduce the heat to low and simmer for 30 minutes or until tender. Drain the lentils and set aside.

5 To make the salsa verde, place the parsley, dill, garlic, lemon zest, capers, olive oil and green peppercorns in a small blender. Add a pinch of salt and a few grinds of pepper. Blend for 30 seconds to form a rough paste. Set aside. (Makes 180 ml.)

6 Remove the shanks from the braising liquid and set aside. Strain the stock, then return it to the casserole and bring to the boil over high heat. Simmer for 30 minutes or until reduced by two-thirds; this should give you a nice rich sauce. Tip the drained lentils into the sauce, then bring to the boil and stir in a generous quantity of the salsa verde.

7 Pour the lentils and sauce over the shanks, then serve with the remaining salsa verde in a bowl to the side.

Veal saltimbocca

Veal saltimbocca is a true Italian classic that matches veal with cured pork and sage. Normally this dish is cooked quickly using the best cuts of veal, which come from the loin and backstrap. However, this is expensive. The tougher – and cheaper – cuts can be used instead and then braised until tender. Italian friends of mine make a braised version that, to be honest, I prefer, so I've included it here. The flavour is terrific and it makes a super winter dish but is also light enough to serve in summer with a crisp salad.

⅓ cup (80 ml) olive oil
½ onion, finely chopped
2 cloves garlic, peeled and finely chopped
1 sprig thyme, leaves picked
2 fresh bay leaves
2 tablespoons tomato paste
2 × 400 g tins chopped tomato
100 ml water
8 slices prosciutto
24 sage leaves
1 × 640 g veal loin, scotch fillet or topside, cut into 8 × 80 g slices
sea salt flakes and freshly ground black pepper

1 Preheat a fan-forced oven to 165°C (185°C conventional).

2 Heat a saucepan over medium heat, then add 30 ml of the olive oil. Cook the onion and garlic for 2 minutes to soften the onion and release the flavour from the garlic. Add the thyme, bay leaves and tomato paste, then stir and cook for a further 2 minutes. Add the tomato and water, then bring to a gentle simmer. Remove from the heat and set aside.

3 Lay a slice of prosciutto on the bench and place 2 sage leaves across the centre. Lay a veal slice on top and fold the prosciutto over the veal, then turn over and set aside. Repeat with the remaining prosciutto, sage and veal.

4 Heat a heavy-based non-stick frying pan over high heat and pour in the remaining olive oil. Working in batches, fry the veal quickly on each side until golden. Remove the veal and place it in an ovenproof frying pan or roasting pan large enough to hold the veal slices in one slightly overlapping layer. Cover with the tomato sauce, then add the remaining sage and seal with a lid or sheet of foil.

5 Bake the veal for 45–60 minutes or until tender. Season the veal saltimbocca with salt and pepper.

Crumbed pork with roasted quince and hazelnuts

Quinces are such a beautiful autumn fruit but, although they have become more popular in recent years, they are still not a regular ingredient in most kitchens. Once you get over the fact that they are very hard and have a velvety fuzz on their thick yellow skins, you will find that they are surprisingly easy to prepare and readily cross the boundary between savoury and sweet dishes. After roasting them, as I've done here, you will be surprised by the result and hopefully inspired to use them more often.

The secret to cooking a good crumbed cutlet is patience. If you start cooking it slowly over low heat and resist the temptation to turn it over before it's time, the crust will brown beautifully.

2 tablespoons hazelnuts
juice of ½ lemon
4 quinces
50 ml olive oil
1½ tablespoons milk
1 free-range egg, beaten
4 pork cutlets, French-trimmed (optional,
    see page 140)
2 tablespoons plain flour
100 g fresh breadcrumbs
20 g unsalted butter
table salt and freshly ground black pepper
2 tablespoons verjuice (see page 141)
baby basil leaves (optional) or watercress sprig
    and lemon wedges, to serve

1 Preheat a fan-forced oven to 180°C (200°C conventional).

2 Roast the hazelnuts on a baking tray for 8 minutes, then transfer to a clean tea towel and rub to remove the skins – don't worry if a little bit of skin remains. Set aside to cool.

3 Squeeze the lemon juice into a bowl of cold water. Peel the quinces quickly with a peeler and cut into quarters. Carefully remove the cores with a paring knife, then place the quince in the lemon water to prevent discoloration.

4 Place an ovenproof, heavy-based non-stick frying pan over medium heat and add a dash of the olive oil. Cook the quince for 3–4 minutes, turning over carefully so it colours lightly and evenly. Transfer to the oven and roast for 15 minutes, turning once or twice until tender.

5 Meanwhile, add the milk to the beaten egg. Coat the pork cutlets with flour, patting off the excess, then coat with the beaten egg mixture and then the breadcrumbs. Pat the cutlets to ensure the breadcrumbs have adhered to the pork.

6 Heat the remaining olive oil in a large heavy-based non-stick frying pan over low heat and pan-fry the cutlets for 6–8 minutes on each side or until golden and crisp.

7 Remove the quince from the oven and place the pan over medium heat, then toss in the hazelnuts and butter. Baste the quince well with the butter and season with a little salt and pepper. Add the verjuice to the pan and reduce until it has almost evaporated. Remove from the heat.

8 Place a pork cutlet on each plate, then place 4 quince pieces neatly around it, sprinkle a few hazelnuts over the quince and drizzle with the pan juices. Sprinkle with baby basil (if using) or watercress and serve with lemon wedges to the side.

Garlicky seafood stew

At its simplest, this lovely Italian fish stew, known as brodetto, contains only one or two types of fish and no shellfish or prawns. The use of fennel, Pernod and dill takes it up a notch and gives the stew a lovely aniseed flavour, which works perfectly with the garlic and sweet fish. Choose meatier fish such as blue-eye trevalla, monkfish or snapper for the body of the meal, as they add flavour and depth, while smaller, more subtle fish such as garfish and red mullet add interest. While fish stock is not essential, starting with a good flavour base contributes to the end result – the better the base the better the stew. Feel free to substitute a good light chicken stock if you prefer.

140 ml extra virgin olive oil
1 onion, thinly sliced
½ bulb fennel, trimmed and thinly sliced
5 cloves garlic, peeled and chopped
pinch of saffron threads
1 tablespoon smoked paprika (see page 140)
6 tomatoes, halved, seeded and roughly chopped
2 sprigs thyme
2 fresh bay leaves
50 ml Pernod
6 waxy potatoes, halved
3 cups (750 ml) Fish Stock (see page 135) or
    Chicken Stock (see page 134)
1 calamari
1 × 200 g blue-eye trevalla fillet, skin removed,
    pin-boned and cut into large chunks
200 g monkfish fillets, skin removed, pin-boned
    and cut into large chunks
200 g red mullet fillets, skin removed, pin-boned
    and cut into large chunks
4 raw prawns
16 clams, soaked in cold water to remove the sand,
    then washed
12 black mussels, well washed, drained
    then bearded
sea salt flakes and freshly ground black pepper
2 tablespoons roughly chopped dill
small handful of roughly chopped flat-leaf parsley
grilled crusty or sourdough bread, to serve

1 Heat 90 ml of the olive oil in a saute pan or large heavy-based saucepan over high heat. Cook the onion, fennel and garlic for 3 minutes or until translucent and tinged slightly golden. Add the saffron and paprika and cook for a further 2 minutes until fragrant, then add the tomato, thyme and bay leaves and cook, stirring, for a few minutes. Add the Pernod and potato, then pour in the stock and bring to the boil. Reduce the heat to low and simmer for 20 minutes or until the potato is tender.

2 Meanwhile, clean the calamari by removing and discarding the skin and contents of the hood. Cut off the tentacles. Wash under cold water, then drain and pat dry with paper towel. Cut the tentacles into 2.5 cm pieces. Cut the hood in half widthways, then thinly slice the hood. Set aside.

3 Add the thickest fish chunks (that is the blue-eye) first, followed by the thinner pieces, then 2–3 minutes later add the prawns. Cover and simmer for 5 minutes, then add the clams, mussels and calamari and cook until the clams and mussels open; discard any unopened ones. Add a pinch of sea salt if required and season with pepper.

4 Throw in the dill and parsley, then add the remaining olive oil. Divide among four bowls and enjoy with grilled bread.

Chilli crab

Take a trip to Singapore or Malaysia and eat chilli crab – forget the shopping and become a food tourist. There is nothing like sitting in thirty degrees Celsius heat with ninety per cent humidity over a bowl of steaming hot (and chilli hot) crab and working your way through the claws, legs and shells with a bib tucked high around your neck. With the sweat beading on your forehead, it's hard work, but it's a great food experience. I have tried many crab recipes with all sorts of sauces, but give me a bib, finger bowl, beer and crab cooked this way and I am a happy man. This recipe for chilli crab is my favourite so I encourage you to give it a go.

2 mud crabs
8 long red chillies
1 onion, roughly chopped
1 piece young ginger
4 cloves garlic, peeled and thinly sliced
90 ml olive oil
1 teaspoon belachan (see page 139)
1 tablespoon coconut vinegar (see page 139)
1 × 400 g tin chopped tomato
2 tablespoons tomato paste
75 g grated palm sugar (see page 140)
200 ml tomato sauce
100 ml soy sauce
1 stick lemongrass, white part only, finely chopped
350 ml water (optional, as needed)
1 free-range egg, lightly beaten
6 spring onions, thinly sliced on the diagonal
small handful of coriander leaves

1 Place the crabs in the freezer to slow their metabolism for 1 hour. Place them top-side down on a chopping board, then quickly cut in half lengthways with a cleaver or large heavy knife. Cut into quarters, then crack the claws with the back of a large knife. Remove the top shell from the body and discard the 'dead man's fingers' (feathery gills that run along either side of the crab's body – you will see them when the top shell is removed).

2 Puree 7 of the chillies, the onion, ginger and garlic in a blender or food processor. Heat a wok over medium heat, then pour in the olive oil. Stir in the onion puree and belachan and cook, stirring, for 3–4 minutes or until fragrant and soft. Stir in the coconut vinegar, tomato, tomato paste and sugar. Simmer for 2 minutes, then add the tomato sauce, soy sauce and lemongrass.

3 Add the crab and bring to a gentle simmer, then cook for 10 minutes or until it is cooked through. Add the water, if required, to keep the mixture loose and bubbling, stirring occasionally.

4 Meanwhile, chop the remaining chilli. Stir in the egg at the last minute until just cooked, add the chopped chilli, spring onion and coriander. Serve with bibs and enjoy!

Prawn laksa

I will travel miles for a good laksa. With all of that coconut cream, chilli oil and the dance of the spices on the palate, it really is an indulgence. I tried my first laksa in Singapore more than twenty years ago. What a sight that must have been – a pasty young Englishman, chopsticks and spoon in hand, bent over a steaming bowl of gorgeousness, slurping, sweating profusely and grinning from ear to ear, like a kid with his first ice cream!

12 raw prawns
⅓ cup (80 ml) vegetable oil
2 tablespoons coriander seeds, crushed
2 teaspoons ground turmeric
2 × 400 ml tins coconut cream
2 cups (500 ml) Chicken Stock (see page 134)
⅓ cup (80 ml) fish sauce
1 tablespoon grated or chopped palm sugar
    (see page 140)
3 stems curry leaves (see page 139)
4 fish balls (see page 140)
8 fried tofu puffs (see page 140)
450 g Hokkien noodles
400 g rice vermicelli noodles
2 large handfuls of bean sprouts
4 spring onions, chopped
deep-fried shallots (see page 139), coriander leaves
    and lime wedges, to serve

LAKSA PASTE
1 thumb-sized piece galangal, peeled and chopped
1 stick lemongrass, white part only, chopped
6 long red chillies, roughly chopped
4 golden shallots, chopped
5 cloves garlic, peeled and chopped
½ bunch coriander, roots only
1 tablespoon belachan (see page 139)

1 To make the laksa paste, start pounding the galangal and then the lemongrass with a mortar and pestle. Add the chilli, followed by the shallot, garlic and well-scrubbed coriander roots and keep pounding. Add the belachan and pound to combine well and form a paste. Set aside.

2 Peel and clean the prawns, leaving the tails intact. Reserve the heads and shells.

3 Heat the oil in a large saucepan over medium heat, then fry the prawn heads and shells for 1 minute or until they turn red. Add the coriander seeds and turmeric and fry for 30 seconds to release their flavours.

4 Add the laksa paste and fry for 5–6 minutes or until fragrant, then add the coconut cream. Continue to cook over low heat for 6–8 minutes or until the oil separates from the cream. Add the stock, fish sauce, palm sugar and curry leaves, then bring to the boil over high heat. Reduce the heat and simmer for 20 minutes. Remove the prawn heads and shells with a slotted spoon and discard. Add the fish balls, fried tofu and prawn meat and cook for 2 minutes over low heat.

5 Meanwhile, blanch the Hokkien noodles and rice noodles separately in boiling water according to the packet instructions, then drain and divide among serving bowls. Pour the laksa over the noodles, then sprinkle with the bean sprouts, spring onion, fried shallots and coriander leaves.

6 Serve with lime wedges.

Swordfish with Iranian figs and green olives

While I love all sorts of olives, I have a soft spot for the big green Sicilian olives. I have used them here as they go brilliantly with the dried figs and a nice piece of swordfish.

95 g dried Iranian figs
boiling water
⅓ cup (80 ml) extra virgin olive oil
1 golden shallot, thinly sliced
½ clove garlic, peeled and sliced
1 cup (250 ml) dry white wine
60 g green Sicilian olives
80 g small caperberries (see page 139)
sea salt and freshly ground black pepper
large handful of flat-leaf parsley leaves,
    coarsely chopped
2 tablespoons olive oil
4 × 120 g swordfish steaks
sea salt and freshly ground black pepper
1 lemon, very thinly sliced
fig vincotto (see page 140), for drizzling

1 Place the figs in a small bowl and cover with boiling water. Leave to stand for 10 minutes, then drain, discarding the water. Pat the figs dry with paper towel, then cut into quarters and set aside.

2 Heat a small saucepan over medium heat, then add 1 tablespoon of the extra virgin olive oil. Cook the shallot and garlic for 2 minutes, stirring regularly; do not allow them to colour. Add the wine and figs, then increase the heat to high and reduce the wine by three-quarters. Remove from the heat and add the olives, remaining extra virgin olive oil and caperberries, then stir to mix. Leave to cool for 5 minutes. Season to taste with salt and a twist or two of pepper. Add the parsley, then stir and set aside.

3 Heat a heavy-based non-stick or enamelled cast-iron frying pan over high heat and add the olive oil. Season the swordfish steaks with salt and pepper, then pan-fry for 2–3 minutes (depending on their thickness) on each side or until tinged a light-golden brown; they are best cooked medium-rare. Remove from the pan and rest for 2 minutes.

4 Place the swordfish steaks on four plates, then spoon over the fig and olive mixture. Divide the lemon among the pieces of fish. Drizzle with a little vincotto and serve immediately.

Barbecued baby snapper

We are truly blessed in this country to have the most delicious types of fish at our fingertips. When the snapper are running hot in Port Phillip Bay it's a bonanza for the amateur fisherman – and us too, of course. Small plate-sized snapper are perfect for cooking whole on the barbecue grillplate. Just make sure the grill bars are super-clean, wipe them with a little oil and have them nice and hot before cooking. Avoid the temptation to turn the fish over too early – it's all about achieving that crisp, slightly charred golden skin.

sea salt flakes
4 × 300 g baby snapper, scaled and cleaned
¼ cup (60 ml) extra virgin olive oil, plus extra
    for greasing and drizzling
freshly ground white pepper
2 stems rosemary, leaves picked
3 tablespoons fennel seeds, lightly crushed
1 teaspoon chilli flakes
1 bunch cavolo nero (see page 139),
    stems discarded
2 handfuls of samphire (optional, see page 140),
    picked over
lemon halves, to serve

1 Preheat a barbecue grillplate on medium heat until nice and hot. Scrub the bars to remove any debris, if necessary, then lightly oil to create a non-stick surface.

2 Bring a large saucepan of water to the boil. Add a good pinch of salt.

3 Remove the fins from the fish with kitchen scissors. Make three 2.5 cm-long × 1 cm-deep incisions on the diagonal on each side of the fish at the thickest part, starting from just behind the gills. Brush the fish with a little olive oil on each side and season with salt, pepper, rosemary, fennel seeds and chilli flakes.

4 Place the fish directly on the hot grillplate. Grill for 5 minutes, then turn the fish over and grill for another 5 minutes or until cooked through. To check whether the fish is cooked, press with your finger on the thickest part just behind the gills: the flesh should give slightly. Alternatively, insert the tip of a knife and have a look: the flesh should be opaque.

5 Meanwhile, cook the cavolo nero and samphire (if using) in the salted boiling water for 2–3 minutes, then drain and drizzle with olive oil.

6 Drizzle the snapper with olive oil, then serve the greens and lemon halves to the side.

Pan-fried barramundi with calamari, tomato and capers   SERVES 2

I love cooking fish. With its delicate flavour and texture, it pairs well with so many other fresh ingredients. Here I have taken barramundi fillets and created a simple, tasty dish in one pan. It's quick and immensely rewarding, which is just how I like to cook when I'm at home.

4 tomatoes
100 g calamari
¼ cup (60 ml) extra virgin olive oil
2 × 150 g barramundi fillets, skin on
sea salt flakes
1 golden shallot, thinly sliced
1 clove garlic, peeled and thinly sliced
pinch of saffron threads
2 anchovy fillets, chopped
50 ml dry white wine
1 tablespoon salted baby capers, rinsed and drained
large handful of baby spinach leaves
freshly ground white pepper

1 Cut a small cross in the base of the tomatoes, remove and discard the cores and place the tomatoes in a large heatproof bowl. Cover with boiling water and leave for 10 seconds. Drain and rinse them with cold water, then peel, remove the seeds and finely chop. Set aside.

2 Clean the calamari by removing and discarding the skin and contents of the hood. Cut off the tentacles. Wash under cold water, then drain and pat dry with paper towel. Cut the tentacles into 2.5 cm pieces. Cut the hoods in half widthways, then cut the calamari into 1 mm-thick strips. Set aside.

3 Heat a heavy-based non-stick frying pan over medium heat, add 1 tablespoon of the olive oil and place the fish gently in the pan, skin-side down. Cook for 3 minutes or until the skin turns golden brown and begins to crisp. Flip over and cook for a further 2 minutes. Transfer the fish to a warmed plate, sprinkle with salt and leave to rest while you make the sauce.

4 Place the shallot, garlic, saffron and remaining olive oil in the same pan. Saute over medium heat for 30 seconds or until softened, then add the anchovies. Cook for another 30 seconds, crushing the anchovies with the back of a fork to release their flavour. Add the wine and reduce for 1–2 minutes or until it has evaporated. Add the tomato and capers and cook for a further 2 minutes or until the tomato softens. Add the calamari and spinach and stir until just cooked, then season with salt and pepper.

5 Divide the sauce among warmed plates, then place a fish fillet on top and serve.

I love a nice fish cake or croquette, all crisp on the outside and soft in the centre. Fish cakes are a great way of using up little bits of fish, or you can use the same quantity of tinned fish or smoked fish such as trout or salmon.

The croquettes can either be deep-fried at 165°C or shallow-fried if you prefer. The prepared croquettes can be placed in an airtight container and stored in the freezer for up to three months. They retain their shape well when thawed, as long as you separate them in the container. If the crumb coating has softened a little, roll them in fresh breadcrumbs before frying.

2 free-range eggs
2 potatoes, peeled
1 × 150 g salmon fillet, skin removed and pin-boned
    (or use tinned salmon)
table salt and freshly ground white pepper
2 tablespoons chopped chervil
2 tablespoons chopped dill
¼ cup (60 ml) milk
½ cup (75 g) plain flour
75 g coarse fresh breadcrumbs
90 ml vegetable or olive oil

GRIBICHE SAUCE
1 free-range egg
200 ml Basic Vinaigrette (see page 136)
4 gherkins, finely chopped
50 g salted capers, rinsed, drained and
    finely chopped
small handful of flat-leaf parsley, finely chopped
small handful of dill, finely chopped
sea salt flakes and freshly ground white pepper

1 Hardboil 1 egg for the gribiche sauce and 1 egg for the fish cakes in a saucepan of simmering water for 9 minutes. Cool, then shell both eggs.

2 To make the gribiche sauce, place the vinaigrette in a bowl, then add the gherkin, capers, parsley and dill. Coarsely grate 1 of the boiled eggs into the sauce. Mix well. Season with salt and pepper to taste and set aside. (Makes about 250 ml.)

3 Put the potatoes into a saucepan and cover with water. Bring to the boil and simmer for 20 minutes or until tender. Drain, then roughly mash and set aside.

4 Steam the fish in a double boiler or a steamer basket over a saucepan of simmering water for 4 minutes. Cool and flake. Set aside.

5 Mash the reserved boiled egg with a fork. Add the fish and the mashed egg to the potato and season with salt and pepper. Add the chervil and dill and mix lightly. Form the mixture into eighteen 5 cm × 1.5 cm croquettes.

6 Lightly whisk the remaining egg and milk together in a shallow bowl, then place the flour and the breadcrumbs in separate flat bowls. Working in batches, coat the croquettes firstly in the flour, gently tapping or shaking to remove any excess, then dip into the egg mixture and drain, and then finally roll in the breadcrumbs. Set aside.

7 Heat the oil in a heavy-based non-stick frying pan and, working in batches, shallow-fry the croquettes over medium heat, turning until golden all over. Remove and drain on paper towel. Serve the hot and crisp croquettes immediately with a bowl of the gribiche sauce.

Spaghetti and meatballs

I love this recipe because as my daughter was growing up, we fed her vegetables in these meatballs and she never knew it. As every parent knows, adding grated zucchini or carrot doesn't always work – the kids find it no matter how small. So make a batch of carrot (as I've done here), sweet potato or cauliflower puree and pop it in zip-lock bags in the freezer for when you need it. Instead of using egg to bind the meatballs, replace it with the puree. The result is soft, sweet and delicious meatballs that are nutritious too!

1 small carrot, finely grated
30 g unsalted butter
100 ml water
400 g minced veal
400 g minced pork
100 g fresh breadcrumbs
small handful of chopped flat-leaf parsley
    (optional)
table salt and freshly ground white pepper
¼ cup (60 ml) extra virgin olive oil
1 onion, finely chopped
2 cloves garlic, peeled and chopped
2 tablespoons tomato paste
2 × 400 g tins chopped tomato
100 ml Chicken Stock (see page 134)
2 sprigs thyme
2 fresh bay leaves
320 g spaghetti
grated pecorino, to serve

1 Cook the carrot, butter and water in a covered saucepan over low heat, stirring occasionally, for 10 minutes or until the carrot is soft (cooking under a tight-fitting lid helps the carrot to cook quickly). Puree in a food processor, then set aside to cool.

2 Mix the minced veal and pork, breadcrumbs, carrot puree and parsley (if using) in a large bowl. Season with 1 teaspoon salt and a little pepper and mould into 2 cm meatballs; you should have 24 meatballs. Set aside.

3 Preheat a fan-forced oven to 165°C (185°C conventional).

4 Heat the olive oil in a large ovenproof non-stick saucepan or enamelled cast-iron casserole. Brown the meatballs over high heat until golden on all sides, then remove and set aside. Fry the onion and garlic for 1 minute or until translucent and soft, then add the tomato paste, tomato and stock. Return the meatballs to the pan, then add the thyme, bay leaves and a little salt and pepper. Bring to a gentle simmer over medium heat, then cover. Cook in the oven for 45 minutes, gently stirring occasionally.

5 Meanwhile, cook the spaghetti following packet instructions in a saucepan of boiling salted water until al dente. Drain. Serve the meatballs with the spaghetti and plenty of grated pecorino.

Linguine with fresh tuna, chilli and garlic

This is one of the simplest pasta dishes you can make. Much like the classic garlic, chilli and parsley sauce, aglio e olio, this one relies on browning garlic and dissolving anchovies in oil to create the flavour base. This dish needs a meaty fish like tuna, swordfish or marlin. The secret to its success is to cook the fish quickly, leaving it pink and moist in the centre – here the tuna is cooked by the residual heat of the pasta and sauce.

The pangrattato, commonly used in the south of Italy, where it is known as 'poor man's parmesan', adds a delicious crunchy topping to this dish.

500 g dried linguine
table salt
100 ml extra virgin olive oil
2 cloves garlic, peeled and sliced
4 long red chillies, thinly sliced
6 anchovy fillets, roughly chopped
1 cup (250 ml) dry white wine
1 × 600 g piece tuna (taken from the top-quarter),
**   cut into 2 cm pieces**
finely grated zest and juice of 1 lemon
2 handfuls of rocket
sea salt flakes and freshly ground white pepper

PANGRATTATO

200g dense sourdough bread,
**   torn into small pieces**
¼ cup (60 ml) olive oil
2 sprigs thyme, leaves picked
sea salt flakes and freshly ground white pepper

1 To make the pangrattato, preheat a fan-forced oven to 180°C (200°C conventional). Place the bread in a heavy-based roasting pan, then drizzle with olive oil. Add the thyme leaves, a good pinch of salt and a few turns of pepper. Toast in the oven for 15 minutes or until golden and crisp, stirring once or twice to ensure the pieces colour evenly. Transfer to paper towel to drain. Set aside until ready to use.

2 Cook the pasta in a large saucepan of boiling salted water for 6–8 minutes or until al dente; stir gently during the first couple of minutes to make sure the pasta doesn't stick together.

3 Meanwhile, heat a deep heavy-based non-stick frying pan or saute pan over medium heat, then pour in half of the olive oil. Add the garlic, chilli and anchovy and cook for 2 minutes or until the garlic browns and the anchovy begins to break up. Add the wine, then bring to the boil and simmer for 2 minutes or until the mixture has reduced by half.

4 Drain the pasta, reserving a little of the cooking water. Tip the pasta into the pan of hot sauce. Add the tuna, lemon zest and juice, rocket and remaining olive oil. Season well with salt and pepper and toss well to mix, adding the reserved pasta water if desired. Sprinkle in half of the pangrattato, then stir once or twice and divide among four bowls. Sprinkle with the remaining pangrattato and serve.

Beetroot risotto with Persian feta

Risotto should be soft and luscious, never thick and stodgy. Most risotto recipes tell you to add a little of the hot stock at a time and stir. With this one, I prefer to add all the boiling stock in one go and only stir it at the end of cooking. I find that this still releases the starch from the rice but keeps the grains intact. The rice should be a touch al dente but never chalky; it is a fine line but once you achieve it your risotto will soar.

For perfect risotto, buy good-quality risotto rice. My first choice is carnaroli, a nice elliptical grain that creates a lovely viscous risotto while maintaining its shape as it absorbs the stock.

2 beetroot
½ cup (150 g) rock salt
500 ml (2 cups) Chicken Stock (see page 134)
60 g unsalted butter, chopped
½ onion, finely chopped
1 clove garlic, peeled and finely chopped
1 teaspoon table salt
200 g carnaroli rice
100 ml dry white wine
freshly ground white pepper
120 g Persian feta
extra virgin olive oil and baby basil (optional),
    to serve

1 Preheat a fan-forced oven to 160°C (180°C conventional). Place the beetroot on a bed of rock salt on a baking tray. Roast for 40 minutes or until tender. Peel and cut one-third of the beetroot into 1 cm dice. Puree the remaining beetroot in a food processor until smooth (you should have 250 ml puree). Set aside.

2 Bring the stock to the boil in a small saucepan over high heat. Melt 30 g of the butter in a shallow wide-based saucepan or non-stick frying pan over medium heat and cook the onion and garlic for 2–3 minutes or until translucent, then add the salt. Add the rice and cook over low heat for a further 2–3 minutes. Add the wine, then allow to reduce, stirring. Add the boiling stock all at once and bring to a simmer; avoid stirring. The stock should be absorbed gradually; this usually takes 15 minutes.

3 After 15 minutes, as the risotto stiffens and absorbs the stock but is still loose, stir in the beetroot puree and cook for a further 2 minutes over low heat. Add the remaining butter and stir in to enrich, then season to taste with salt and pepper.

4 Spoon the risotto onto four plates, tapping each one to flatten it a little. Crumble over the feta and sprinkle with a few pieces of beetroot, then dress with a little olive oil. Sprinkle over baby basil leaves (if using) and serve.

Saffron risotto with clams and lemon mascarpone

If you are looking for the perfect mid-week meal in a bowl, risotto hits the spot. The addition of saffron and mascarpone give this one a very special flavour.

500 g clams or pipis, soaked in cold water to remove the sand, then washed
¼ cup (60 ml) olive oil
2 cloves garlic, peeled and finely chopped
1 onion, finely chopped
4 sprigs thyme
200 ml dry white wine
2 cups (500 ml) Chicken Stock (see page 134), approximately
90 g unsalted butter, chopped
sea salt flakes
1 cup (200 g) risotto rice, such as carnaroli
2 good pinches of saffron threads
2 tablespoons mascarpone
2 tablespoons thickened cream
freshly ground white pepper
grated zest of ½ lemon
small handful of flat-leaf parsley, chopped
extra virgin olive oil, to serve
thyme leaves and flowers (optional), to serve

1 Place a large stainless-steel saucepan with a lid over high heat and heat for 1 minute. Meanwhile, drain the clams. Remove the lid from the pan and add 1 tablespoon of olive oil. Add half of the garlic and onion. Quickly add the clams and thyme, stir once, then add 100 ml of the white wine and put the lid on the pan. Cook for 2–3 minutes or until the clams have popped open. Remove from the heat and drain in a colander with a bowl underneath to catch all the juices. Set the juices aside. Leave the clams to cool for a few minutes, then pick the meat from three-quarters of the shells and set aside. Discard the empty shells, onion, garlic and thyme.

2 Place the stock and the reserved shellfish juices in a large saucepan over high heat and bring to the boil. Melt 30 g of the butter in a wide, shallow non-stick saucepan over medium heat and cook the remaining garlic and onion for 2–3 minutes or until translucent, then add 1 teaspoon of salt. Add the rice and cook over low heat for 2–3 minutes. Add the saffron and stir through the rice, then pour in the remaining white wine and stir for 1–2 minutes until reduced by half. Add three-quarters of the hot stock all at once and bring the rice to a simmer; avoid stirring too often. The stock should be absorbed gradually – it usually takes 15 minutes.

3 Meanwhile, place the mascarpone and cream in a small stainless-steel bowl, add a pinch of sea salt and a twist of pepper, then add the lemon zest and whisk for 30 seconds until soft peaks form. Set aside.

4 As the stock is absorbed into the rice, stir in the remaining stock, if required, until you have a soft yielding risotto with a tiny amount of bite to the grains. Add the remaining butter and stir to incorporate. Add the clams in the shell and clam meat to the risotto and stir through gently. Turn the heat off and leave to sit for a minute for the heat to draw through the clams. Stir in the mascarpone mixture at the last second, along with the parsley.

5 Spoon onto plates, tapping to flatten a little. Drizzle with extra virgin olive oil, scatter with thyme leaves and flowers (if using) and serve.

SWEET THINGS

Profiteroles with chocolate and hazelnut cream

During a recent trip to Paris I was reminded of how what once was old can indeed be new again. I found incarnations of these little choux creations in patisseries everywhere.

⅓ cup (90 g) chocolate and hazelnut spread
¾ cup (180 ml) mascarpone
1 cup (250 ml) thickened cream, whipped

SABLE PASTRY
100 g chilled unsalted butter, chopped
50 g icing sugar, sifted
table salt
125 g plain flour, sifted, plus extra for dusting
1 free-range egg yolk

CHOUX PASTRY
135 ml milk
105 ml water
table salt
100 g unsalted butter, chopped
135 g plain flour
1 teaspoon caster sugar
3 free-range eggs, plus 1 free-range egg yolk

1 To make the sable pastry, cream the butter and sugar, then add ¼ teaspoon of salt. Add the flour and mix to combine, then add the egg yolk. Continue mixing until the dough is smooth. Turn the dough out onto a floured bench, sprinkle it with a little more flour and bring together with your hands into a ball, kneading gently once or twice. Flatten with your fingers until 2 cm thick, then wrap in plastic film. Refrigerate for 20 minutes.

2 Sprinkle the dough with a little flour, then roll it between two sheets of baking paper until 1 mm thick. Refrigerate for 15 minutes, then mark out twenty-four 4 cm squares with a large knife.

3 To make the choux pastry, bring the milk, water, 1 teaspoon of salt and the butter to the boil in a heavy-based saucepan over high heat. Add the flour and sugar and, using a wooden spoon, stir for 1 minute or until the mixture thickens and starts to pull away from the side of the pan. Reduce the heat to medium, then cook the mixture for a further 3–4 minutes, stirring constantly; it should pull away from the side of the pan and be quite smooth. Remove the pan from the heat and leave the mixture to cool for 5 minutes. Add 1 egg at a time and beat with a wooden spoon; the pastry should be smooth after adding each egg. Add the egg yolk and beat until the pastry is smooth and shiny, then transfer it to a piping bag fitted with a 1 cm nozzle and set aside.

4 Preheat a fan-forced oven to 180° (200°C conventional).

5 Line two baking trays with baking paper. With the tip of your finger, smear a little of the choux pastry on the corner of each tray to help the paper stick. Pipe the choux pastry onto the trays to form 4 cm rounds, leaving a 2.5 cm gap between them. Cut out the 4 cm squares of sable pastry, then gently lay a square onto each choux round. Bake for 15 minutes, then reduce the oven temperature to 160°C (180°C conventional) and bake for another 15 minutes. Transfer the choux buns to a wire rack and leave to cool.

6 Mix the chocolate and hazelnut spread and mascarpone together in a medium-sized bowl and set aside in the fridge.

7 Prepare two piping bags, each fitted with a 5 mm nozzle. Place the whipped cream in one and the chocolate and hazelnut cream in the other. Make a hole in the side of each bun with the tip of a small knife. Fill half of each bun with the whipped cream and the other half with the chocolate and hazelnut cream. Serve.

Dark chocolate souffles with milk chocolate ganache

You can't beat a great chocolate souffle. Every time I put them on the menu of one of my restaurants, the chefs look at me as if to say, 'boring', yet the dessert flies out the door. Dish up these babies at a dinner party and you'll be a kitchen god or goddess.

2 teaspoons cornflour
2 teaspoons plain flour
2 tablespoons Dutch-process cocoa (see page 140), plus extra for dusting
1 tablespoon caster sugar
4 free-range egg yolks
200 ml milk
100 g dark couverture chocolate (70 per cent cocoa solids, see page 139), broken into small pieces, plus 50 g extra, finely grated
25 g unsalted butter, softened, for greasing

MERINGUE
8 free-range egg whites
140 g caster sugar

MILK CHOCOLATE GANACHE
100 ml thickened cream
100 g milk chocolate, broken into small pieces

1 To make the ganache, bring the cream to the boil in a small heavy-based saucepan, then add the chocolate. Leave for 30 seconds, then stir with a flexible spatula (see page 140) until smooth. Cool, then cover with plastic film and refrigerate for 30 minutes or until firm. Beat the ganache for 20–30 seconds with the spatula to lighten. Cover and return to the fridge until needed.

2 To make the souffles, sift the cornflour, plain flour and cocoa into a mixing bowl, then add the caster sugar and mix well. Add the yolks to the flour mixture and whisk with a balloon whisk (see page 139) until smooth.

3 Bring the milk to the boil in a small heavy-based saucepan. Pour half of the hot milk over the egg yolk mixture, then whisk briskly for a few seconds to combine. Transfer the egg yolk mixture to the pan of remaining warm milk and return to medium heat. Whisk to combine, then cook, whisking continuously to prevent lumps from forming and the mixture from catching on the base, for 3 minutes or until it comes away cleanly from the side of the pan. Remove the pan from the heat, then add the chopped chocolate and stir to melt. Transfer the mixture to a clean bowl, press a piece of plastic film directly onto the surface and set aside until cool.

4 Brush the inside of eight 225 ml-capacity (or four 350 ml-capacity) ramekins well with butter. Refrigerate for 10 minutes. Butter lightly again and dust with the grated chocolate.

5 Preheat a fan-forced oven to 180°C (200°C conventional).

6 To make the meringue, whisk the egg whites until soft peaks form, then gradually add the sugar and whisk until firm peaks form. (Do not over-beat the egg white after adding the sugar or it will become cloudy and you'll beat all the air out trying to remove the lumps.)

7 Gently fold one-third of the meringue into the chocolate mixture with a flexible spatula to form a smooth, soft batter. Add the remaining meringue, turning the bowl and folding in the meringue simultaneously. Spoon the mixture into the ramekins, filling evenly to the top of each one; do not spill it over the side or the lip as this can make the batter stick and prevent the souffles from rising.

8 Bake the souffles for 12 minutes (15 minutes for larger ramekins) or until the tops are 2.5 cm above the ramekins. Remove the ganache from the fridge.

9 Remove the souffles from the oven, dust with extra cocoa and serve immediately, topped with a spoonful of ganache.

Chocolate fudge

I took inspiration for this chocolate fudge recipe from the old cookbook that came with my grandmother's Radiant stove when she bought it in the 1940s. Things really don't change much, do they? It's important to work quickly with this recipe. When the mixture has cooled and you begin to beat the fudge, it will thicken and stiffen. The mixture should still be at a consistency where it can be poured easily, otherwise it will be too stiff and difficult to work with. For best results, you'll need to use a sugar thermometer (see page 141).

1 teaspoon vegetable oil, for greasing
300 ml milk
2 cups (400 g) soft brown sugar
1 × 395 g tin condensed milk
100 g unsalted butter, chopped
1 teaspoon vanilla extract
⅓ cup (35 g) Dutch-process cocoa
 (see page 140)

1 Grease a baking tin (mine is 22 cm × 16 cm × 4 cm) with oil, then line with baking paper, pressing in with your fingertips (leave enough overhanging to allow the fudge to be easily removed from the tin).

2 Place the milk and sugar in a large heavy-based saucepan and leave to stand for 1 hour, stirring occasionally.

3 Add the condensed milk, butter, vanilla extract and cocoa to the pan. Place the pan over medium heat, stirring the mixture frequently as it comes to the boil; the mixture will be light and bubbling. Simmer the fudge mixture for 15–20 minutes, stirring frequently to prevent the mixture from sticking to the base of the pan, until it begins to thicken and registers 120°C on a sugar thermometer. Remove from the heat and leave the fudge mixture to cool in the pan for 5 minutes.

4 It is important to work quickly at this stage. Using a wooden spoon, stir and beat the fudge mixture vigorously for 30 seconds or until it thickens and slightly loses its gloss. Quickly pour the fudge mixture into the prepared tin and smooth the surface with a wet palette knife (see page 140). Leave at room temperature for 1 hour or until the fudge has set.

5 Using the overhanging baking paper, lift the fudge from the pan, then remove the baking paper. Cut the fudge into squares and store in an airtight container for up to 3 days. Do not refrigerate.

Apple tarte tatin

Starring soft caramelised apples and a slightly bitter, deep-amber caramel, this has to be my favourite apple tart. It was invented in the 1880s by two unmarried sisters who ran the Hotel Tatin in the Loire Valley, France, apparently by mistake – and what a mistake it was! Thank you to the Tatin sisters and bon appetit!

375 g prepared butter puff pastry, thawed
7 granny smith apples, peeled, quartered
**   and cored**
finely grated zest and juice of 1 lemon
200 g caster sugar
70 g unsalted butter, chopped
creme fraiche or ice cream, to serve

1 Preheat a fan-forced oven to 180°C (200°C conventional).

2 Roll out the puff pastry into a round that it is 2–3 cm bigger than an ovenproof 26 cm cast-iron frying pan. Prick the pastry all over with a fork and place it on a baking tray in the fridge to rest. Meanwhile, mix the apple with the lemon zest and juice and set aside.

3 Cover the base of the frying pan with the sugar and top with the butter. Place the pan over high heat and stir for 4 minutes or until the sugar and butter turn a light-caramel colour. Remove the pan from the heat. Place the apples on top of the caramel in concentric circles, starting from the outside of the pan and working your way into the centre. Lay the pastry on top of the apples and use a spoon or your fingers to push the pastry down around the apples against the edge of the pan (effectively tucking them in as if with a blanket).

4 Bake the tart for 35 minutes or until the pastry is a deep golden-brown. Remove the pan from the oven and set aside for 10 minutes. Place your hand on the top of the pastry and gently rotate the tart a few centimetres to ensure it has not stuck to the base of the pan. If it has, put the pan back into the oven for 2 minutes to melt the caramel a little.

5 Place a plate over the tart and invert the pan in one smooth movement so that the pan is now on top. Lift off the pan to reveal the tart. Serve slices of the tarte tatin with a generous dollop of creme fraiche or ice cream.

Classic creme brulees

Creme brulee is a classic French bistro dessert best shared at a slightly cramped table as waiters bustle by, barking at each other in French. Failing that, make it at home to remember the reason you like to order it in restaurants in the first place, as you smell the scent of burning sugar wafting through your kitchen. To achieve the perfect caramelised sugar crust, you need to burn a scattering of sugar on the surface of each one, hence the 'brulee' part of the title, which means 'burnt' in French. You will need a small butane blowtorch from a kitchen equipment store or hardware store, if all else fails – it won't be as fancy but it will do the job.

1 vanilla pod, split
1 litre pouring cream
255 g caster sugar
12 free-range egg yolks

1 Preheat a fan-forced oven to 140°C (160°C conventional).

2 Scrape the vanilla seeds into a large bowl, then add the cream, 180 g of the sugar and the egg yolks and whisk together.

3 Divide the mixture between six 250 ml-capacity brulee or souffle moulds. Place the moulds into a large roasting pan. Take the pan to the oven, then fill it with boiling water halfway up the side of the moulds. Bake for 45 minutes. Chill the brulees in the fridge.

4 Just before you are ready to serve them, sprinkle the surface of each custard evenly with 1 tablespoon sugar. Use a blowtorch to melt and caramelise the sugar, then serve.

Panna cotta with roasted apricots and honey

The secret to a good panna cotta is using the best-quality cream you can buy, then using just enough gelatine to hold it all together. As you turn out the panna cotta it should bow and bulge under its own weight. Soft, luscious and irresistible.

2 cups (500 ml) thickened cream
½ vanilla pod, split
60 g caster sugar
1½ leaves titanium-strength gelatine
   (see page 140)
olive oil, for greasing

ROASTED APRICOTS AND HONEY
20 g unsalted butter
1 stick cinnamon
2 star anise
4 cloves
6 apricots, halved and stoned
dash of apricot liqueur
⅓ cup (120 g) honey

1 Place the cream, vanilla and sugar in a saucepan and bring to the boil, then remove from the heat. Meanwhile, soak the gelatine leaves in cold water until soft. Squeeze the leaves, then stir through the hot cream mixture until dissolved. Strain the liquid through a fine-mesh sieve into a heatproof jug.

2 Oil six 100 ml-capacity dariole moulds very lightly with a little olive oil using the tip of your finger. Pour one-sixth of the cream mixture into each mould, then leave to set in the fridge for at least 6 hours or overnight.

3 Preheat a fan-forced oven to 180°C (200°C conventional).

4 To make the roasted apricots, place a heavy-based ovenproof frying pan over medium heat for 1 minute, then add the butter, cinnamon, star anise and cloves and allow the butter to melt and bubble. Place the apricots cut-side down into the pan and fry gently for 3–4 minutes or until golden. Turn the apricots over, then transfer the pan to the oven to roast for 4–5 minutes or until the apricots are just soft. Remove from the oven, then add the apricot liqueur and drizzle with honey. Leave the apricots to cool in the pan for 5–10 minutes.

5 To unmould the panna cotta, gently tease the edge of each dariole mould to release, then turn upside-down onto a bowl or plate. Place 2 apricot halves next to each panna cotta and drizzle with the syrup from the pan, then serve.

Sweet cheese crumble souffles with blackberries

These souffles are by far the lightest 'cheesecake' you will ever eat. The secret to achieving a perfect souffle lies in buttering the mould properly so it rises above the rim rather than catching on the sides. There will be extra crumble mixture leftover, which can be baked on top of your favourite fruit.

25 g soft unsalted butter, plus extra for greasing
¼ cup (35 g) plain flour
3 free-range eggs, separated
160 g caster sugar, plus extra for dusting
finely grated zest of 1 lemon
½ cup (125 ml) milk
125 g cream cheese
½ vanilla pod, split and seeds scraped
icing sugar, for dusting
ice cream, to serve

CRUMBLE
50 g cold unsalted butter, chopped
½ cup (75 g) plain flour
50 g soft brown sugar

BLACKBERRIES
250 g blackberries
⅓ cup (75 g) caster sugar

1 Mix the butter and flour in a small bowl until a paste forms. Whisk the egg yolks with 40 g of the sugar in another bowl until pale and creamy, then add the lemon zest and set aside. Place the milk, cream cheese and vanilla seeds in a saucepan and whisk over low heat until the mixture is smooth and begins to boil. Whisking continuously, add tablespoonfuls of the butter mixture to the milk mixture until thick and smooth. Whisk for another 3 minutes, then remove from the heat. Whisk in the egg yolk mixture and combine well. Transfer to a bowl, cover closely with plastic film to avoid a skin forming, then set aside to cool.

2 To prepare the blackberries, place them and the sugar in a small stainless-steel saucepan, then stand for 10 minutes. Simmer over low heat for 3–4 minutes; the berries should be soft but still hold their shape. Remove from the heat and set aside.

3 Grease four 250 ml-capacity souffle moulds well with extra soft butter, then refrigerate for 10 minutes. Grease again with butter lightly but evenly, then sprinkle each mould evenly with 1 tablespoon of the extra sugar and shake out the excess.

4 Preheat a fan-forced oven to 180°C (200°C conventional).

5 To make the crumble, rub the butter into the flour until the mixture resembles coarse breadcrumbs, then add the sugar. Spread the mixture over a baking tray and bake for 5 minutes or until light golden. Cool and set aside.

6 Using a whisk or hand-held electric beaters, whisk the egg whites with 60 g of the caster sugar until soft peaks form. Slowly add the remaining 60 g sugar and beat for another minute or until stiff and glossy. Using a large metal spoon, fold one-third of the egg white mixture into the souffle base to loosen it, then fold in the remaining egg white mixture.

7 Place 1 tablespoon of the blackberries in the base of each prepared souffle mould, then spoon one-quarter of the souffle mixture evenly on top. Place the moulds on a baking tray and bake for 12 minutes or until risen and golden.

8 Sprinkle the souffles with a little of the crumble mixture, dust with icing sugar and top with a spoonful of blackberries. Serve with the extra berries and ice cream to the side.

Zabaglione with raspberry puree

Those clever Italians – imagine creating a gorgeous dessert from nothing more than egg yolks, sugar, a little sweet wine and a great deal of panache! Making zabaglione (and its French counterpart, sabayon) is not easy. Don't let the temperature get away from you. If it does, then simply remove the bowl from the pan of simmering water. Continue whisking, then feel the bottom of the bowl. Is it still hot enough to cook the egg? If not, pop the bowl back over the simmering water and continue to whisk.

750 g raspberries
juice of ½ lemon
2 teaspoons pure icing sugar
5 free-range egg yolks
⅓ cup (80 ml) white dessert wine
**   (such as botrytis)**
80 g caster sugar
ice cubes
⅓ cup (95 g) natural Greek-style yoghurt

1 Puree 500 g of the raspberries in a food processor with a good squeeze of lemon juice and the icing sugar. Push through a fine-mesh sieve into a bowl, pressing down with the back of a ladle to extract as much juice as possible, then discard the seeds and set aside.

2 Fill a saucepan one-third-full with water and bring to the boil over high heat. Place the egg yolks, wine and caster sugar in a large heatproof bowl that fits snugly over the saucepan without the base touching the simmering water. Using a balloon whisk (see page 139), whisk the mixture until light and airy for about 30 seconds.

3 Place the bowl over the simmering water (ensuring the bowl does not touch the water), then heat the mixture, whisking continuously, for 8–10 minutes or until it is very light and holds its shape. When the mixture thickens and falls back on itself (it should form ribbons when you lift the whisk above the bowl), you'll know it is ready. Remove the bowl from the pan of water and place over a bowl of iced water, then continue to whisk until the mixture is cool. (Alternatively, whisk in the bowl of an electric mixer until cool.) The mixture will become viscous, shiny and more stable.

4 Fold the yoghurt into the zabaglione. Just before serving, carefully pour enough of the raspberry puree into the zabaglione to create a swirl. (Serve the leftover puree alongside or store in an airtight container in the fridge for up to 3 days.)

5 Scatter over the remaining raspberries and serve immediately.

Ricotta pancakes with date and banana butter

Ricotta pancakes have been on the breakfast menus of my restaurants since day one. While there is always a place for thin pancakes or crepes, thick pancakes are the go for a hearty and satisfying breakfast. There's nothing better than sitting down to a plate of fluffy pancakes with a latte in your hand, the gentle warmth of the morning sun and the promise of an easy hour to read the Sunday paper – ah. Wake up Gary, you're dreaming again, the kids are screaming and it's time to get a move on!

1⅔ cups (250 g) self-raising flour
pinch of table salt
50 g caster sugar
1 free-range egg
300 ml milk
25 g unsalted butter
75 g firm ricotta, drained and crumbled
vegetable oil or extra butter, for cooking
maple syrup or caster sugar and lemon wedges
    (optional), to serve

DATE AND BANANA BUTTER
125 g unsalted butter, chopped and softened
75 g dates, pitted and chopped
2 small bananas, mashed

1 To make the date and banana butter, whip the butter with hand-held electric beaters until light and creamy, then stir in the dates and banana. Set aside.

2 To make the pancakes, sift the flour and salt together, then add the sugar. In another bowl, whisk the egg and milk together, then add to the flour mixture. Beat well with a whisk to remove any lumps.

3 Melt the butter in a frying pan over low heat until it bubbles and becomes nut-brown. Whisk the burnt butter into the batter, then stir in the ricotta; don't worry if there are a few lumps.

4 Heat a heavy-based non-stick frying pan over medium heat with a drizzle of oil or knob of butter. Place a small ladleful of the batter in the hot pan and cook for 2–3 minutes. When bubbles appear on the surface, gently turn the pancake over and cook for another 2–3 minutes. Transfer the pancake to a plate and repeat with the remaining batter. You should end up with 8 pancakes.

5 Serve the pancakes with the date and banana butter and maple syrup, or with extra sugar and lemon wedges, if using.

Jam roly-poly with custard

Jam roly-poly reminds me of my childhood – I can't resist it. Mum used to make a great jam roly-poly with loads of her own strawberry jam and thick custard. I hope I have done her proud.

Making your first real custard is a bit of a thrill because it is so easy and tastes brilliant in comparison to the packaged stuff (and everyone will think you are pretty clever!).

You will need a steamer insert that fits snugly over a saucepan to cook roly-poly. If you don't have one, a bamboo steamer is the perfect substitute – cheap and easy to use.

1⅓ cups (200 g) self-raising flour
30 g caster sugar
200 g suet mix (see page 141)
200 ml water (approximately)
plain flour, for dusting
60 g good-quality strawberry jam

CUSTARD
2 cups (500 ml) milk
½ vanilla pod, split
5 free-range egg yolks
90 g caster sugar
⅓ cup (50 g) cornflour

1 Mix the self-raising flour, sugar and suet mix in a large bowl with your hands. Make a well in the centre and pour in the water, then gently draw the flour into the centre with your fingers. It may need a little extra water, so judge this yourself – you are looking for a soft-textured dough. The secret is not to overwork the dough. Turn the dough onto a lightly floured surface and gently shape it into a ball. Press the dough down with your fingers to create a rectangular shape, then transfer it to a 60 cm × 60 cm sheet of baking paper. Dust with a little flour and roll it out until it is 1 cm thick, leaving a 6 cm border of paper.

2 Use a spatula to spread the dough liberally with jam, leaving the top 3–4 cm jam-free. Wet this top edge with a little water. Starting at the bottom edge, start to roll the pastry away from you all the way to the top. Slide the jam roly-poly back towards you until it reaches the bottom edge of the baking paper. At this point, slide the baking paper and jam roly-poly onto a clean tea towel. Roll it all up loosely; this allows the pastry to expand during cooking. Tie the ends of the tea towel together with kitchen twine to seal.

3 Place the jam roly-poly in a saucepan steamer insert. Fill the saucepan with 4 cm water, then bring to the boil over high heat. Place the steamer insert on top of the pan, then cover with the lid and steam for 45 minutes.

4 To make the custard, bring the milk and vanilla pod to the boil in a saucepan. Meanwhile, whisk the egg yolks and sugar until pale and fluffy, then whisk in the cornflour. Pour the hot milk into the egg mixture, then pour the lot back into the saucepan and whisk continuously over high heat until it thickens.

5 To check if the roly-poly is ready, insert a skewer into the centre of the roll – it should come out clean and feel hot. Remove the roly-poly from the steamer, then unwrap it and cut it into slices. Serve slices of the roly-poly with lashings of custard.

6 If your steamer is not big enough, you can make two small roly-polys instead; just be sure to reduce the cooking time accordingly, checking them after 25 minutes.

Rich creamy rice pudding with strawberry jam

SERVES 4

I love a bowl of creamy rice pudding. This version is from my days in The Connaught Hotel kitchens in London. It is extra-rich and super-smooth, and it is almost impossible not to go back for seconds.

When I revisit this recipe it always surprises me how much milk the rice absorbs, so remember to stir it regularly over the lowest possible heat and avoid adding the sugar until the end as it inhibits the cooking process and may make the rice burn more easily.

1 cup (200 g) short-grain rice
850 ml milk, plus 150 ml extra if needed
½ vanilla pod, split
3 free-range egg yolks
100 g caster sugar
⅓ cup (110 g) good-quality strawberry jam

1 Place the rice, milk and vanilla pod in a large heavy-based saucepan. Bring to the boil, then simmer over low heat for 45 minutes or until the rice is tender. Stir regularly, otherwise the milk and rice will stick to the base of the pan and may burn; add a little more milk if required to keep the mixture soft and creamy.

2 As the rice becomes soft towards the end of cooking (after about 40 minutes), whisk the egg yolks and sugar in a bowl until pale and creamy. Remove the rice from the heat and pour it into the bowl of egg mixture, then combine, stirring quickly with a flexible spatula.

3 Serve the hot rice pudding in bowls, topped with a dollop of strawberry jam.

Plum tart with pistachio crumble

A frangipane (almond cream) filled tart is timeless and just perfect when served while it's still warm. All kinds of fruits, such as stone fruits and berries, work brilliantly in this tart.

180 g unsalted butter, softened
180 g caster sugar
3 free-range eggs, plus 1 yolk
a few drops of almond essence
finely grated zest of 1 lemon
180 g ground almonds
60 g plain flour
2 tablespoons pistachio paste (optional, available from specialty food stores)
6 small plums, pitted and halved

SWEET SHORTCRUST PASTRY

125 g unsalted butter, softened
30 g icing sugar
240 g plain flour
table salt
1 free-range egg

PISTACHIO CRUMBLE

3 cups (750 ml) water
½ cup (75 g) shelled pistachios
30 g chilled butter, chopped
40 g caster sugar
40 g plain flour

1 To make the sweet shortcrust pastry, place the butter in the bowl of an electric mixer fitted with a paddle attachment. Add the icing sugar and mix until creamy, then add the flour and a pinch of salt. Mix for 30 seconds, then add the egg and continue to mix for 10 seconds or until the dough comes together to form a ball. Flatten the dough gently into a disc with your fingers. Wrap in plastic film and rest in the fridge for 20 minutes. Tear off two 40 cm sheets of baking paper.

2 Remove the dough from the bowl and roll out between the baking paper until 3 mm thick, then line a tart tin with a removable base (mine is 28 cm-long) with the pastry. Peel off one sheet of the baking paper, then invert the pastry over the tin, gently laying it in the tin. Remove the second sheet

of baking paper and mould the pastry up the sides of the tin with your fingertips. Remove any excess pastry with your thumb by pressing down along the edges of the tin. Refrigerate for 30 minutes.

3 Preheat the oven to 180°C fan-forced (200°C conventional).

4 To make the pistachio crumble, bring the water to the boil in a small saucepan over high heat. Sprinkle the pistachios into the pan and simmer for 1 minute, then remove from the heat. Drain the pistachios and place on a clean tea towel. Using the tea towel, gently rub off the skins. Pat the peeled pistachios dry, then pulse in a food processor to form a course meal. Transfer to a bowl, then add the butter, sugar and flour and rub together with your fingertips to combine roughly. Set aside.

5 Line a small baking tray with baking paper and sprinkle the crumble mixture onto the tray, then bake for 10 minutes or until golden. Set aside to cool.

6 Press a sheet of baking paper onto the pastry, then fill with baking beads, dried beans or rice and bake for 12 minutes. Remove the weights and baking paper and bake the pastry for another 5 minutes or until it is golden and dry. Set aside.

7 Using an electric mixer, cream the butter and sugar together until creamy, then, with the motor running, add the eggs and egg yolk, one at a time, continuing to mix after adding each one. Add the almond essence, lemon zest, ground almonds, flour and pistachio paste (if using) and mix to incorporate.

8 Pipe or spoon the almond mixture into the tart shell to reach the top of the tart tin, then level the surface with the back of a spoon. Gently press the plum halves into the almond mixture, placing them at even intervals along the tart. Bake the tart for 30 minutes or until golden.

9 Remove the tart from the oven and leave to cool. Sprinkle the crumble generously over the tart and serve.

Lemon curd mousse with gingernut crumble

I have never been a big fan of cheesecake, especially the baked variety – I find them too heavy and claggy. On the other hand, this recipe is a beauty, turning the traditional idea of cheesecake on its head, with a fluffy, light and citrus-y cream cheese filling on the bottom, topped with a crisp crumble 'base'.

150 g cream cheese, at room temperature
1 cup (250 ml) double cream
200 g condensed milk
finely grated zest and juice of 1 lemon
finely grated zest and juice of 1 lime
chopped pistachios, to serve

LEMON CURD
¾ cup (180 ml) lemon juice
finely grated zest of 1 lemon
5 free-range eggs
¾ cup (165 g) caster sugar
125 g unsalted butter, chopped

GINGERNUT CRUMBLE
65 g unsalted butter, chopped and softened
50 g soft brown sugar
1 tablespoon treacle
1 free-range egg yolk
1¼ cups (185 g) self-raising flour, plus extra
**   for dusting**
½ teaspoon bicarbonate of soda
1 tablespoon ground ginger
1 teaspoon ground star anise
1 teaspoon ground cinnamon

1 Preheat a fan-forced oven to 180°C (200°C conventional).

2 To make the crumble, beat the butter, sugar, treacle and egg yolk in a bowl until combined. Add the flour, bicarbonate of soda, ginger, star anise and cinnamon. Using your hands, combine the ingredients to form a firm dough. Turn the dough onto a lightly floured surface, then rub through with your fingertips to make large 'crumbs' and spread onto a baking tray lined with baking paper. Bake for 8 minutes or until golden. Remove from the oven and set aside to cool.

3 To make the lemon curd, place the lemon juice, zest, eggs, sugar and butter in a microwave-proof bowl and microwave on medium for 6–8 minutes, stopping to stir regularly until the mixture is thick. Transfer to a clean airtight container and seal. Lemon curd will keep in the fridge for up to 2 weeks. (Makes 250 ml.)

4 Whisk the cream cheese in a large bowl until soft and smooth, then add the cream and condensed milk and whisk until thick and creamy; the longer you whisk, the lighter and creamier it will be. Add the citrus zest, juice and 150 ml of the lemon curd and whisk for a few seconds only.

5 Spoon the mousse into six glasses, sprinkle with the gingernut crumble, top with a few chopped pistachios and serve.

Summer trifle with berries and crunchy meringues

Trifle was always a standby for Mum when we had visitors over summer and it's a standby for me today because it is so versatile.

This is a brilliantly easy dessert that appeals to the soul and makes the most of summer's berries. It's my take on the great Aussie pav in the form of a trifle with berries and cream. Doesn't get any better than this!

250 g strawberries
150 g raspberries
150 g blackberries
⅔ cup (150 g) caster sugar
200 g mascarpone
200 ml pouring cream
1 vanilla pod, split and seeds scraped
10 amaretti biscuits
75 ml Amaretto

CRUNCHY MERINGUES
6 free-range egg whites
250 g caster sugar

1 Preheat a fan-forced oven to 130°C (150°C conventional). Line a baking tray with baking paper.

2 To make the meringues, whisk the egg whites and sugar in a stainless-steel bowl for 5–10 minutes with hand-held electric beaters until the mixture is silky and stiff peaks form. Transfer to a piping bag fitted with a 1 cm plain nozzle, then pipe 1.5 cm wide × 1.5 cm high meringues out onto the baking paper. Bake for 45 minutes or until crisp on the outside and still soft in the centre. (Makes about 30.)

3 Bring half of the berries and the caster sugar to the boil in a small saucepan over medium heat. Simmer for 6 minutes or until the sugar dissolves and the berries collapse. Puree the berry mixture in a blender.

4 Whisk the mascarpone, cream and vanilla seeds with hand-held electric beaters until soft peaks form, then set aside. Crush the biscuits and drizzle with the Amaretto.

5 Spoon or pipe a little of the berry puree into the base of four glasses, then spoon in some of the cream mixture. Add some of the berries and a little more cream, then add a layer of biscuits. Repeat this layering process until all the cream mixture, berry puree, berries and biscuits are used. Pile a few meringues high on each trifle and serve.

Raspberry sorbet

Ices are always a winner for dessert. Restaurateurs also love them as they form such an integral part of more complicated desserts on their menus – I couldn't live without them.

Sorbet can become icy and hard if left in the freezer for a long time (that is, several days or weeks). It is best to transfer it from the freezer to the fridge to soften for 30 minutes before serving.

150 ml water
⅔ cup (150 g) caster sugar
finely grated zest and juice of 1 lemon
400 g frozen or fresh raspberries

1 Bring the water and sugar to the boil in a small saucepan over high heat. Remove the sugar syrup from the heat and set aside to cool.

2 Blend the lemon zest, juice and raspberries in a blender or food processor until smooth, then add the sugar syrup and blend for another 30 seconds to incorporate. Push the puree through a fine-mesh strainer or sieve over a bowl to remove the seeds.

3 Pour the mixture into an ice cream machine and churn until thick and smooth, following the manufacturer's instructions. If you don't have an ice cream machine, place the sieved raspberry mixture in a bowl in the freezer for a couple of hours, whisking every 45 minutes or so until frozen.

4 Blend in a food processor quickly to break up the icy lumps and return to the freezer for several hours to freeze into a sorbet. Serve scoops of sorbet in bowls or glasses.

Lemon sorbet

Lemon sorbet is surprisingly simple to master. It's amazing that fresh lemons, sugar and water can be combined to create something that tastes so heavenly and is so refreshing. Remember that much of the flavour of lemon comes from the oil in the zest. Take care to grate the zest and leave the bitter white pith behind.

1 cup (250 ml) strained fresh lemon juice
finely grated zest of 2 lemons
1 cup (250 ml) sparkling mineral water
1 free-range egg white

HEAVY SUGAR SYRUP
400 g caster sugar
400 ml water

CANDIED LEMON SLICES (OPTIONAL)
100 g white sugar
100 ml water
1 lemon, cut into 2 mm-thick slices

1 To make the heavy sugar syrup, place the sugar and water in a small heavy-based saucepan and bring to a simmer over low heat. Remove from the heat, then set aside to cool. Refrigerate until chilled (domestic ice-cream machines work more efficiently if the liquid is chilled first). (Makes 400 ml).

2 Mix together the lemon juice, lemon zest, mineral water and sugar syrup.

3 Churn the mixture in an ice-cream machine following the manufacturer's instructions. When nearly set, remove 3 tablespoons of the sorbet and, using hand-held electric beaters, whisk in the egg white until it is foamy.

4 Add the mixture to the ice-cream machine and continue to churn until you are happy with the consistency. (Sorbet will keep in an airtight container in the freezer for up to 1 month.)

5 To make the candied lemon slices (if using), place the sugar and water in a small saucepan, then slowly bring to the boil over medium heat. Reduce the heat to low, then add the lemon slices and simmer for 10 minutes. Remove from the heat and leave to cool. (Store in an airtight container in the fridge for up to 1 month.)

6 Serve scoops of the sorbet in glasses or bowls, topped with candied lemon slices (if using).

BASICS

Chicken stock

This chicken stock is a white chicken stock, as it is based on raw bones. Chicken stock does not require a long cooking time – it is all about preserving the fresh flavour of the chicken, vegetables and aromats.

1 kg free-range chicken bones, chopped
    into 5 cm pieces
2 litres water
1 stick celery, finely chopped
1 onion, finely chopped
½ bulb garlic, peeled
1 fresh bay leaf
2 sprigs thyme
8 white peppercorns

1 Bring the chicken bones and water to the boil in a heavy-based stockpot over high heat. Skim any impurities from the surface and discard. Add the celery, onion, garlic, bay leaf, thyme and peppercorns. Gently simmer the stock over low heat for 2 hours, skimming the surface once or twice to remove the fat.

2 Turn off the heat and leave the stock to cool for approximately 40 minutes. Strain the stock through a fine-mesh sieve, discarding the bones and vegetables, then leave to cool completely. Transfer the stock to airtight containers, then seal, label and date. Store in the fridge for up to 5 days or freezer for up to 2 months.

Beef or veal stock

This is called a brown stock because it is based on beef bones that are first roasted and caramelised before being slowly simmered with the other ingredients.

1 kg beef or veal bones, cut into 3–4 cm pieces
50 ml olive oil
1 stick celery, cut into 2.5 cm pieces
1 carrot, cut into 2.5 cm pieces
1 onion, cut into 2.5 cm pieces
1 head garlic, halved widthways
2 litres water
8 sprigs thyme
2 fresh bay leaves

1 Preheat a fan-forced oven to 180°C (200°C conventional).

2 Place the beef or veal bones in a large heavy-based roasting pan, drizzle with the olive oil and roast for 1 hour or until golden. Turn the bones regularly to ensure they colour evenly. Add the vegetables and garlic to the pan, then roast for a further 10 minutes, turning the vegetables once or twice to ensure they colour evenly.

3 Transfer the bones and vegetables to a large stockpot, then cover with the water. Bring to the boil over high heat, then skim any impurities from the surface and discard. Add the thyme and bay leaves. Simmer over low heat for 8 hours, skimming impurities from the surface of the stock regularly.

4 Turn off the heat and leave the stock to cool for approximately 40 minutes. Strain the stock through a fine-mesh sieve, discarding the bones and vegetables, then leave to cool completely. Transfer the stock to airtight containers, then seal, label and date. Store in the fridge for up to 5 days or freezer for up to 2 months.

Fish stock

Fish stock adds a lovely depth of flavour to seafood-based dishes such as risotto, soups and, of course, fish sauces.

1 kg white fish bones (no heads) such as snapper, whiting or blue-eye trevalla, chopped along the spine into 4–5 sections.
1 tablespoon olive oil
1 small leek, white part only, halved lengthways, washed well and thinly sliced
1 small bulb fennel, trimmed and thinly sliced
1 small onion, thinly sliced
2 star anise
4–5 sprigs thyme
1 bay leaf
1 teaspoon sea salt flakes
1 teaspoon white peppercorns
100 ml dry white wine
2 litres water

1 Wash the fish bones under cold running water for 1–2 minutes to remove any blood and impurities. Drain and set aside.

2 Heat the olive oil in a stockpot over medium heat, then add the fish bones and the rest of the ingredients except the wine and water. Cook for 3 minutes or until the spices release their aroma. Add the wine, then bring to the boil and pour in the water. Bring to the boil, skimming any impurities from the surface as it begins to boil. Reduce the heat to low and simmer for 20 minutes.

3 Remove the stock from the heat and leave to stand for 5 minutes. Strain carefully into a large bowl through a fine strainer or muslin cloth, then cool quickly. Transfer the stock to airtight containers, then seal, label and date. Store in the fridge for up to 4 days or freezer for up to 2 months.

Basic mayonnaise

There is nothing quite like making your own mayo. Try using different vinegars and mustards, such as wholegrain or sweeter styles for variation.

2 free-range eggs
2 tablespoons dijon mustard
1 tablespoon white balsamic vinegar
1 teaspoon table salt
600 ml olive oil

1 Blend the eggs, mustard, vinegar and salt in a blender or food processor until creamy. Add 300 ml of the olive oil and blend until creamy. Add the remaining oil and continue blending until creamy. Store, closely covered with plastic film, in the fridge for up to 5 days.

Basic vinaigrette

It is very easy to make your own vinaigrette – just experiment with a variety of different oils, vinegars, herbs, spices and mustards until you find a combination you like. As long as you follow the basic rule of thumb, one part acid to two parts oil, you can't go wrong.

2 teaspoons Dijon mustard
1 teaspoon honey
finely grated zest and juice of ½ lemon
2 tablespoons white balsamic vinegar
table salt and freshly ground white pepper
¾ cup (180 ml) olive oil

1 Whisk the mustard, honey, lemon zest and juice and balsamic vinegar together. Add a pinch of salt and pepper. Drizzle in the olive oil, whisking continuously to emulsify. Store in an airtight container in the fridge for up to 2 weeks.

GLOSSARY

Balloon whisk
The curved edge of this teardrop-shaped whisk conforms perfectly to the interior shape of mixing bowls, making it ideal for incorporating air into egg whites or cream.

Belachan
Otherwise known as shrimp paste, this stinky, salty paste is made from fermented dried prawns or krill pressed into blocks. Widely used across South-East Asia, from Indonesia, Thailand and Malaysia through to Vietnam and southern China, it adds saltiness and complexity to dishes. It is generally roasted, grilled or fried before it is added to a dish. Available from Asian food stores and larger supermarkets.

Caperberries
The edible bud and fruit of the caper bush, preserved in vinegar. Available from specialty food stores.

Cavolo nero
A dark long-leafed cabbage with a deep earthy flavour. If unavailable, substitute silverbeet or kale.

Chinese sausage (lap cheong)
A sweet, red, dried pork sausage. There are several different varieties. They are quite hard but develop a lovely flavour when sliced and steamed, grilled or fried on their own or as part of more complex dishes. Available from Asian food stores and larger supermarkets.

Coconut vinegar
Coconut vinegar is a cloudy white vinegar made from fermented coconut water or sap from the coconut tree. It has a lovely balance of acidity and adds interest and complexity to dishes. Available from Asian food stores.

Cornichons
These small crisp cucumbers are generally picked when 3–4 cm long, then pickled in brine. Available from specialty food stores and delicatessens.

Couverture chocolate
Chocolate must contain a minimum of 32 per cent cocoa butter and a 54 per cent combined total of cocoa solid and cocoa butter to be graded as couverture. The higher percentage of cocoa butter and solids a chocolate contains, the less sugar it has, and, as a result, the more chocolate-y the flavour.

Curry leaves
These fragrant little leaves grow on a small tropical tree. They're used to impart a curry-like flavour to dishes. Available fresh or dried from select greengrocers and spice stores.

Deep-fried shallots
Finely chopped and deep-fried red shallots add a lovely crisp texture and depth of flavour to all sorts of Asian dishes. Available from Asian food stores and larger supermarkets.

Duck fat
French food and duck fat go hand in hand. It used to be hard to get hold of duck fat but it can now be purchased in tins from good delis or specialty food stores, although it can be expensive. Luv a Duck produce one in Australia – the quality is good, but use it sparingly. Duck fat can be rendered at home by mincing and placing it in a saucepan over low heat with a little water to start the process off. Slow-cooking clarifies the fat and the water evaporates, leaving the clear fat. The secret to keeping duck fat for a long period is to separate the fat from any moisture or natural stock that may be emitted when you cook with it. The fat may also sour if you handle it with your hands. If you keep out any moisture and always use a clean spoon, the duck fat will keep in the fridge for several weeks.

Dutch-process cocoa
Cocoa is the powder remaining after the cocoa butter has been extracted from cocoa beans. Dutch-process cocoa is unsweetened cocoa treated with an alkali to neutralise its acids, resulting in a more rounded chocolate-y flavour.

Fig vincotto
A condiment made from cooked grape must and figs. Available from specialty food stores and good delis.

Fish balls
Fish-based meatballs are popular street food in China, Singapore, Thailand, Malaysia and the Philippines. Available in the fridge or freezer section of Asian food stores.

Flexible spatula
This flexible semi-rectangular spatula with rounded edges is often made from rubber or heat-resistant silicone. It's the tool of choice for mixing ingredients, folding batters (such as cake batters), spreading batter evenly in the pan and icing cakes.

French-trimming
This is a decorative way of presenting a piece of meat (such as cutlets and shanks) with a piece of bone protruding that has been stripped of all fat, sinew or skin.

Fried garlic
Crispy fried garlic is widely available from Asian grocers. It can be bought sliced, nibbed or broken. It adds a lovely texture and flavour to all sorts of Asian dishes from fried rice to soups and salads.

Fried tofu puffs
These packaged deep-fried tofu pieces are available from the fridge section of Asian food stores.

Gelatine leaves
Available as titanium, platinum or gold strength, gelatine leaves are pure and easy to use. Commercial kitchens generally avoid using powdered gelatine because leaf gelatine has better setting properties so the results are more predictable. Available from specialty food stores and good delis.

Palette knife
A long-handled utensil with a rounded, blunt blade that is used for turning food being cooked in a pan, removing food from baking trays and spreading icing, cream or ganache over cakes.

Palm sugar
Palm sugar is made from the sap of the sugar palm tree. Usually sold in rock-hard cakes, the sugar is shaved off with a sharp knife or box grater (though many good-quality Asian palm sugars are softer). Available from Asian food stores and larger supermarkets.

Panko breakcrumbs
These large Japanese-style dried breadcrumbs are popular because they remain light and crisp when fried. Available from Asian food stores and larger supermarkets.

Samphire
A salty, edible coastal plant, often called sea asparagus, with small, smooth, juicy buds that branch out. If unavailable, substitute any meaty leafy green, such as kale, silverbeet or cabbage.

Simmer mat
Also called a heat diffuser, this is placed between the heat source and the pan to regulate low heat and prevent food from sticking to the base of the pan.

Smoked paprika
This has become increasingly popular over the last few years as it adds a fantastic smoky and complex flavour. Deep-red in colour, a good smoked paprika is slowly smoked over oak and sold in three varieties – hot, bittersweet and sweet. The best brands, such as La Chinata, come from La Vera in Spain. It can be used with care in any dish where you might use a sweet or mild paprika. Available from specialty food stores and good delis.

Suet mix
Available from the baking or spice section of the supermarket as a flour or suet mixture. Fresh suet (raw beef or mutton fat) is a different product that needs to be ordered in advance from a butcher. If you wish to use fresh suet instead, freeze it and

then grate it into a bowl. Rub in an even quantity of flour with your fingers until it comes together to form a texture similar to coarse breadcrumbs, then proceed with the recipe.

Sugar thermometer

Used to measure the temperature of sugar when making sugar syrups, caramel and confectionery. It can also be used to test whether jam has reached setting point and the temperature of oil for deep-frying.

Sumac

This ground deep-red spice is made from a slightly astringent red berry commonly used in Middle Eastern cooking. Available from spice stores.

Verjuice

Verjuice is made from under-ripe, unfermented grapes. It has been used in cooking in the grape-growing regions of the world for hundreds of years. It can be used in dressings, sauces and marinades and in any dish that needs a dash of acidity. It can replace other sour flavours such as lemon, lime and vinegars. Available from specialty food stores.

Yellow rock sugar

A dark yellow sugar that is a crystallised form of a mixture of honey, refined and unrefined sugars. Available from Asian food stores and larger supermarkets.

Index

LANTERN

Published by the Penguin Group
Penguin Group (Australia)
707 Collins Street, Melbourne, Victoria 3008, Australia
(a division of Pearson Australia Group Pty Ltd)
Penguin Group (USA) Inc.
375 Hudson Street, New York, New York 10014, USA
Penguin Group (Canada)
90 Eglinton Avenue East, Suite 700, Toronto, Canada ON M4P 2Y3
(a division of Pearson Penguin Canada Inc.)
Penguin Books Ltd
80 Strand, London WC2R 0RL, England
Penguin Ireland
25 St Stephen's Green, Dublin 2, Ireland
(a division of Penguin Books Ltd)
Penguin Books India Pvt Ltd
11 Community Centre, Panchsheel Park, New Delhi – 110 017, India
Penguin Group (NZ)
67 Apollo Drive, Rosedale, North Shore 0632, New Zealand
(a division of Pearson New Zealand Ltd)
Penguin Books (South Africa) (Pty) Ltd
24 Sturdee Avenue, Rosebank, Johannesburg 2196, South Africa

Penguin Books Ltd, Registered Offices: 80 Strand,
London, WC2R 0RL, England

First published by Penguin Group (Australia), 2012

10 9 8 7 6 5 4 3 2 1

Text copyright © Gary Mehigan 2012

Photographs copyright © Dean Cambray
(pages 9, 11, 12, 15, 19, 27, 31, 53, 57, 58, 61, 65, 66, 73, 74,
77, 79, 89, 90, 93, 95, 106, 109, 117, 119, 121, 125, 127, 129)

Photographs copyright © Mark Chew
(pages 17, 23, 41, 45, 47, 50, 55, 63, 71, 81, 85, 87, 101, 103,
105, 114, 122, 130)

Photographs copyright © Simon Griffiths
(pages 20, 25, 28, 33, 35, 36, 39, 49, 69, 82, 97, 111, 113)

Photographs copyright © Adrian Lander
(pages 2, 137, 138)

Design by Lantern Studio © Penguin Group (Australia)
Typeset in Alright Sans and Adobe Caslon
by Post Pre-press Group, Brisbane, Queensland
Colour reproduction by Splitting Image, Clayton, Victoria
Printed in China by Everbest Printing Co Ltd

National Library of Australia
Cataloguing-in-Publication data:

Mehigan, Gary.
Lantern cookery classics : Gary Mehigan / Gary Mehigan

9781921383151 (pbk.)
Includes index.

Cooking.

641.5

penguin.com.au/lantern

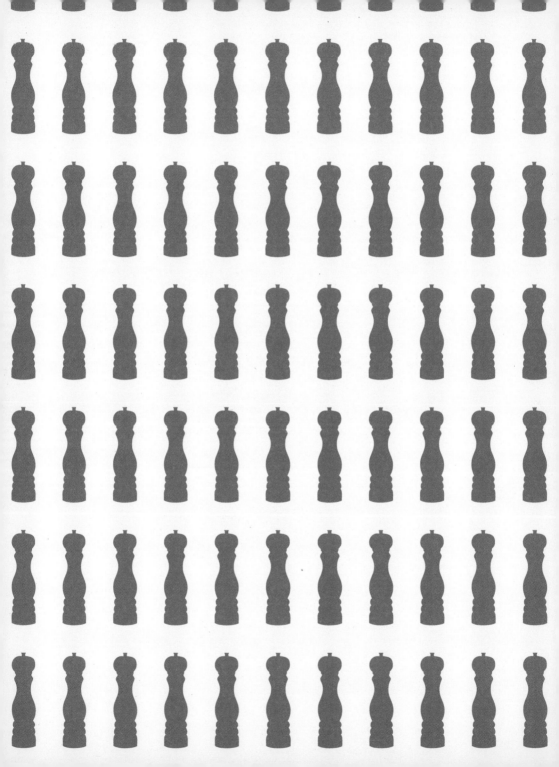